ROUGH
OFF ROAD BIKE R

CW00481563

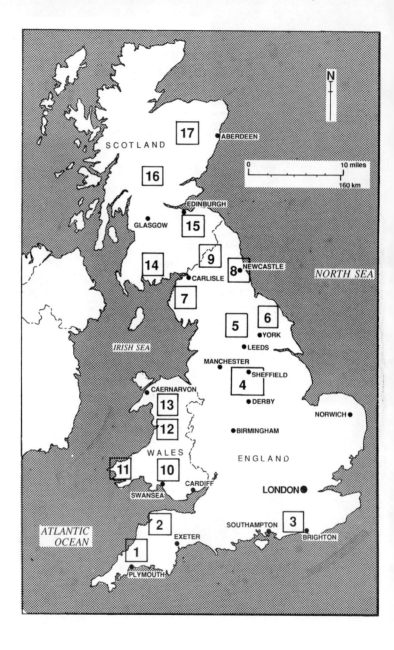

ROUGH RIDES

Off-Road Bike Routes in Britain

David Robinson & John Holmes

MPC

Published by:
Moorland Publishing Co Ltd,
Moor Farm Road West,
Ashbourne,
Derbyshire DE6 1HD
England

First published 1990
Revised second edition 1992

British Library Cataloguing in
Publication Data
A catalogue record for this book is
available from the British Library.

ISBN 0 86190 189 4

Black & White origination by:
Monochrome Scanning Ltd
Printed in the UK by:
Billings & Son Ltd, Worcester

Cover picture: A. Fearn.

Photographs have been supplied as
follows:
Dumfries & Galloway Tourist
Board: p149; A. Fearn: pp52, 132
(both), 143, 185; J. Moss: p79;
MPC Picture Collection: pp 45, 63;
Perthshire Tourist Board: pp 169,
171; D. Robinson: pp 26, 38, 65, 90,
95, 100, 104; Scottish Borders
Tourist Board: pp 157, 162; L.
Smith: p177; Wales Tourist Board:
pp 109, 115, 125; West Country
Tourist Board: pp 18, 32; Yorkshire
& Humberside Tourist Board: p 71.

Contents

Acknowledgements

In the research and writing of this book I would like to extend my very special thanks to those people who have helped me make this project come true.

Those thanks go to John, Lynda, Laura and Richard who helped so much with the routes in Scotland and the North-East. I would also like to thank Alan Fearn for taking the cover shots (excellent job Al) and for coming along with me from time to time in the cool spring evenings to set up and take many other creative photographs.

Thanks also go to Dawes Cycles of Birmingham for providing me with a superb bike which coped brilliantly throughout and certainly came into its own on the most difficult sections; to Brooks for supplying the saddles for both John's and my bike; and to Andre of Cyclone in Belper who generously supplied me with protective head gear.

I finally completed the book, John. Many thanks for your research, route planning in Scotland and encouragement throughout . . . .on yer bike!

David Robinson

Key to Maps

— — — Off road track	▬▬▬▬▬ Main road
➤ ➤ Direction of route	───────── Minor road
	══════ Motorway

Note on Maps

The maps in this guide are not designed to be used as accurate route maps, but rather to help readers plan ahead.

For more detailed maps, it is recommended that you use the Ordnance Survey's Landranger map series as this forms the basis for the routes described in the book.

Introduction

When an experienced mountain biker and photojournalist get together you will almost inevitably end up with a book on mountain biking. However, from the time this book was first conceived, around Christmas 1989, it soon became evidently clear that there was much more work involved than selecting a few off road rides, testing them and writing a detailed account of them.

Once suitable areas of Britain had been chosen, several evenings were spent gazing at the many maps needed, trying to plan routes from each region; routes that would provide a variety of potentially good tracks for *Rough Rides*.

Driving hundreds of miles all over the country to spend 2 or 3 days at a time, testing the routes and seeking out places of interest to visit was obviously the most enjoyable part of the research involved. The process included driving to an area, locating the starting point, riding along the selected route, navigating and making notes.

This book is aimed at the tourist and not just the rider. We have included places of interest that are worth parking your bike for as well as a variety of places to stay.

The routes cover quiet country lanes, tracks of varying quality and bridleways, which are often neglected. We have attempted to rate the rides into three categories, but these are only personal judgements and should not be necessarily interpreted as any kind of official grading system for mountain biking.

At least three routes are suggested in most areas. They vary in length and in the time that they will take. We have, as far as possible, attempted to return to the original starting point, which is often situated near a place of refreshment.

Some of the rides will take you only 3 or 4 hours, others may be a day trip. Whichever the ride, take your time and explore some of the superb areas of Britain's countryside.

This guide should not be followed religiously. Using the book and a map, plan your route before you set out — making alterations as you wish. The maps provided in this guide are not intended as accurate route maps, but to enable you to plan ahead. The detailed maps recommended should always be used, together with the route descriptions. If, for example, you do not fancy the suggested bridleway, select an alternative route or, if you would rather spend more time in the forest, work at some suitable extensions.

Do bear in mind that you are allowed to cycle on bridleways, but **not** public footpaths and that in England and Wales you must avoid private land. However, the laws in Scotland are slightly more complex. Basically there are no trespass laws, but as cyclists, who by their very nature care about the environment, you should respect other people's land.

The book has been written with the desired intention of making mountain biking more popular by using the routes that are accepted by all, not by riding rough-shod over the countryside leaving devastation in your wake.

It is presumed that the reader has some experience of cycling so there is no great detail about how to mend a puncture or how to choose a bike the right size. However, if you are thinking of buying a mountain bike for the first time, do not pay too much attention to the paintwork and the aggressive sounding names, look instead at the frame and its components. Seek advice from the cycle dealer and not the brochure. Before you open your cheque book get a second opinion and go for a ride to be sure of what you are buying.

We both ride Dawes cycles, using Reynold's 531 Magnum The Edge for most of these routes. It has proved to be ideal for the varying terrain up and down the country; being strong, light, reliable and fairly quick. The saddle is also an important feature of the bike and, opting for comfort, we have found the Brook's leather saddle to be most suitable.

Once you have bought your bike, then buy a helmet. Make sure that the helmet meets either of the two American standards, Snell and ANSI, Z90.4 as well as the British Standard BS6863.

Chapter 1

Bodmin

Bodmin and the North Cornish Coast were selected as the most south-westerly region for off road cycling in Britain. The bleak, barren hills of Bodmin Moor and the rugged cliffs and sandy coves of the wave-lashed coastline certainly provide contrasting and dramatic scenery.

The North Cornish coastline is perhaps best known for its dramatic cliffs and sandy beaches. If you have had to travel a long way to get to Cornwall you will certainly want to see some of this coastal scenery, so by including two routes along the coastal region we hope to have provided a fair indication of the area and landscape. It is also an exhilarating experience to ride close by the coast and to be able to constantly gaze out to sea.

Bodmin Moor is about 20km (12 miles) from north to south and 18km (11 miles) from east to west. It is crossed by only one major road, the A30 from Launceston to Bodmin. The first impressions gained are of a remote and desolate place where you would not wish to be in bad weather. Few lanes enter the heart of the moor, and its most remote parts can only be reached on foot, horseback or mountain bike.

Much of the moor consists of rough and rolling moorland, bogs, marshes, rocky outcrops and ancient stones. However, towards the borders of the moor, the land is more gentle and here rivers tumble from the granite plateau through wooded valleys on their course to the sea.

Two of the highest peaks, Rough Tor and Brown Willy, are sited on the northern part of the moor. Looming large on the south-east moor are Kilmar Tor, overlooking Twelve Mens Moor, and Stowes Hill, with the strange rockpile known as the Cheesewring on its western slopes.

Bodmin and Tintagel are the centres from which the rides in this region start and it is really your decision as to where you choose to be based. Whether you prefer the coast or somewhere inland, there are literally hundreds of places to stay.

The central and northern part of Cornwall seems to offer the best off road cycling and, looking at the map, Bodmin Moor is an obvious choice. However, north of the A30 the few tracks that lead onto the moor are dead ends and it has not proved possible to incorporate a circular ride in this part. If you have time, though, you may choose to follow one or two of these narrow lanes and tracks to reach the highest peaks and visit some of the ancient stone remains.

Places to Stay

Allegro Hotel
50 Higher Bore Street
Bodmin
PL31 1JW
☎ 0208 3480

Mount Pleasant
  Farm/Guest House
Mount Village
Bodmin
PL30 4EX
☎ 0208 82342

The Mill House Inn
Trebarwith
Tintagel
☎ 0840 770200

Westberry Hotel
Rhind Street
Bodmin
PL31 2EL
☎ 0208 2772

Trewarmett Lodge Hotel
  and Restaurant
Trewarmett
Tintagel
☎ 0840 770460

Places of Interest

*Bodmin and Wenford
  Railway*
Bodmin
☎ 0208 77963

This is a small country railway terminus situated between two lines of track to Bodmin Parkway and Boxcarne Junction. Steam-hauled brake van rides can be taken along the 10km (6 miles) of track. Also worth visiting is the museum, although this is only open on certain days (phone for further details). The railway is open May to September.

*Duke of Cornwall's
Light Infantry
Museum*
The Keep
Victoria Barracks
Bodmin
☎ 0208 72810

This is a military museum containing weapons, medals, uniforms and battle relics covering the regiment's history from 1702 to the present day.
Open: all year Monday to Friday. Closed Bank Holidays.

Tintagel Castle
Tintagel
☎ 0840 770328

A medieval ruined castle sited high on the cliffs of the wild, windswept coast. It is famous for its associations with Arthurian legend. The castle dates back to the thirteenth century, having been built by Richard, Earl of Cornwall.
Open: daily Easter to September and Tuesday to Sunday from October to Easter.

Throughout this region some of the most interesting places to visit and things to see are found either on Bodmin Moor or the coast. On Bodmin Moor, for example, there are countless relics which include the Stripple Stones on the southern slopes of Hawks Tor Downs; a circular earthern mound enclosing a few remaining standing stones, one an ancient temple dating back about 4,000 years ago. The Hurlers near Minions, Goodaver near Dozmary Pool and King Arthur's Hall, 3km (nearly 2 miles) south-west of Rough Tor, are three of the many stone groups scattered over the moor.

Being one of Britain's favourite holiday regions, the coast boasts some fine, rocky scenery and clean, sandy beaches and coves. Attractive, unspoilt villages, both along the coast and inland, offer plenty for the visitor to enjoy.

North Cornwall Ride 1

56km (35 miles)
Landranger Map 1:50,000 Sheet 200
Starting Point: Nanstallon (Bodmin) Map Ref 040 670

Brief Description

Quite an easy route on mostly good quality narrow lanes and dismantled rail tracks along a beautiful section of the Cornish coastline and through the quiet, rolling hills of this part of the country.

The Route

Leave Nanstallon on the narrow lane that runs just south of the River Camel. Turn right, crossing over the river to Boscarne. From Boscarne turn left onto a dismantled rail track and follow this as it runs alongside the river for about 8km (5 miles) to Wadebridge.

Cross over the A39 to join the Wadebridge to Padstow Path and follow this for 9km (5$^1/_2$ miles) to Padstow. Go through Padstow to join a lane that goes past the Bird Garden towards Trethillic, and eventually turns into a track leading towards the coast. At the end of this track head for Trevone and, on passing through the village, turn right onto the B3276 for a short distance before turning right again to Harlyn. Just past Harlyn you come to a T-junction where you turn right. Follow the narrow road round as it bends to the left. A short excursion to Trevose Head is well worth a visit to sample this part of the beautiful North Cornish Coast.

Continue southwards past Treyarnon to join the B3276 near Porthcothan and stay on this coast road now for 5km (3 miles) until you come to Trenance. This is a really lovely section of the route giving fine views over the coastline. Once past Trenance take the narrow lane which heads east along the Vale of Mawgan. You pass just across the top of St Mawgan and all the way to St Columb Major.

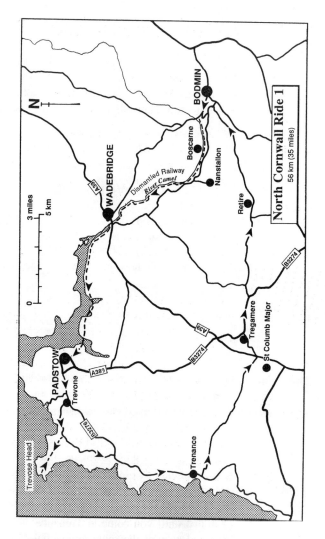

North Cornwall Ride 1
56 km (35 miles)

There is a choice of points where you can then cross the A39 from St Columb Major to join a lane which leads to Tregamere. From there turn left and then right onto the B3274. Stay on the B-road for 2km (1¼ miles) until it bears sharp right. At this point take the narrow and hilly lane that leaves the B3274 and heads in a more or less straight line eastwards in the direction of Bodmin. After 5km (3 miles) you come to a T-junction by the tiny place called Retire. Turn left and continue for a further 5km (3 miles) passing Tremore, Lower Woodley and back into Bodmin.

North Cornwall Ride 2

58km (36 miles)
Landranger Map 1:50,000 Sheet 200
Starting Point: Tintagel Map Ref 060 885

Brief Description
A mildly difficult ride on dismantled rail track and some very hilly country lanes. This is a very attractive route in a quiet region of Cornwall, especially by the coast and particularly the resort of Tintagel.

The Route
Leave Tintagel on the B3263 heading south. After 1$\frac{1}{2}$km (1 mile) you come to a sharp bend on the left. Turn sharp right just past this into a lane which drops very sharply past Treknow keeping right on down to the crossroads. Go over the crossroads and climb quite steeply along the lane that leads to Westdowns in 3km (2 miles). At the junction of the B3314 turn right and immediately left and after about 1km ($\frac{2}{3}$ mile) join the dismantled rail track and head right for just over 6km (3$\frac{3}{4}$ miles) leaving the track just east of St Kew. The track passes under a few lanes and accurate map reading is called for if you plan to follow this route accordingly.

Ride along the country lanes heading west into St Kew and continue to Trewethern and St Minver. Once through St Minver you can follow the right fork to Dolzeath or, for

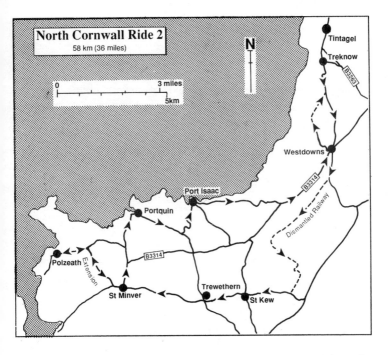

North Cornwall Ride 2
58 km (36 miles)

0   3 miles
    5km

N

Tintagel
Treknow
B3263
Westdowns
B3314
Dismantled Railway
Port Isaac
Portquin
Polzeath
Extension
B3314
Trewethern
St Minver
St Kew

an alternative part of the coast, then head north from St Minver for 3km (nearly 2 miles) to Portquin. The route from here on zig-zags between the coast and just a few kilometres inland. The coastal path is a footpath which cyclists are not allowed to use. Therefore, follow the narrow lane as it bends round from Portquin only slightly inland before heading back to the coast at Port Isaac. There is a very steep descent into the small resort and quite a steep climb out as the lane follows the line of the coast for a short distance before veering east to join the B3314.

Turn left onto the B-road to Westdowns taking the lane on the left across the hillside back to Treknow and Tintagel.

Ruins at
Tintagel

Bodmin Moor Ride

58km (36 miles)
Landranger Maps 1:50,000 Sheets 200 and 201
Starting Point: Turfdown (east of Bodmin) Map Ref 095 658

Brief Description *A fairly easy ride over narrow country lanes and forest tracks around the beautiful Bodmin Moor. There are several hills which may prove steep at times but should not present any problems.*

The Route Although this ride actually starts from Turfdown, to get there from Bodmin follow the A389 to the A30 at Carminow Cross. Take the A38 from the roundabout and first left after $1/_2$km ($1/_3$ mile) along the narrow road to Turfdown. Go over the railway to the T-junction. Turn

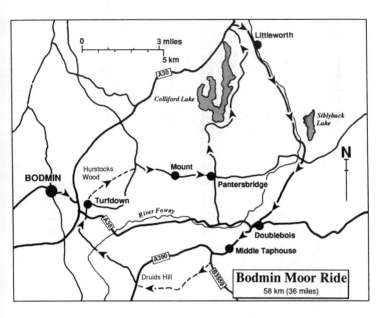

right and immediately left to follow a very narrow lane that leads into the forest ahead. The lane becomes a well defined track as you head through Hurstocks Wood. Keeping to the right side of the wood, about half way through, follow the track which forks right and out of the wood to join the narrow lanes again.

At the crossroads go straight over and follow the road for Mount. Go over the crossroads heading eastwards all the time and onto Pantersbridge. Go through this village and in 2km (1$\frac{1}{4}$ miles) you come to a crossroads on the Goonzion Downs. Turn left there to climb for about 3km (nearly 2 miles) to Colliford Lake. Fork right, riding past the southern end of the lake, crossing the bridge over the St Neot River and continue up the eastern side of the lake to join a track on the right just past Dozmary Pool. Follow this track which drops down into Littleworth and turn right onto the lane which runs alongside the River Fowey.

Continue along this narrow lane for 6km (3$\frac{3}{4}$ miles) as it cuts through this bleak but most attractive section of the Cornish moorland. As you approach Trekeivesteps bare sharp right to climb the slope. You actually follow the hill round for only a short distance before descending gradually to a T-junction where you turn right and head for Doublebois.

At Doublebois go over the crossroads to join the B3360 and the A390 to Middle Taphouse. Turn left onto the B3359 and after 1km ($^1/_2$ mile) a track forks to the right and into the woodland. There are a few options in the woodland but try to keep fairly central, aiming for Druids Hill in the western part. You will eventually come out onto the A390 close by Druid's Hill. Cross over the main road to join the narrow lane which leads across the hills and goes over the rail line just south of Bodmin Parkway Station and towards the A30. Turn right just before the A30 and head back to Turfdown or Bodmin, depending on where you started.

Chapter 2

Exmoor

Exmoor is one of the smallest national parks in Britain. It stretches 430km (265 miles) across the borders of West Somerset and North Devon from Dulverton northwards to the Bristol Channel and from Combe Martin eastwards to Minehead.

Huge sea cliffs tower majestically over the Bristol Channel with a spectacular coastline of hogsbacked headlands offering superb views across to the distant Welsh mountains.

Inland, the very heart of Exmoor is a remote, bleak and empty wilderness of wild heather moorland and green plateaux with deep wooded valleys that carve their way through this forbidding landscape.

In the east, rising from the Vale of Porlock, the Brendon Hills give way to a less intense landscape, gentle valleys, farmland and an area that is inhabited. Exmoor's many attractive villages include Parracombe, with its stone cottages, and Dunster, famous for its castle and medieval timbered houses.

Undoubtedly Exmoor is a region of outstanding natural beauty. Thinly populated, but rich in wildlife, Exmoor is famous for its wild red deer. The national park has the second largest herd outside Scotland. Next to the deer, Exmoor's second most famous animal is the Exmoor pony. Foxes, badgers, ravens, buzzards and otters can also be seen. Care should be taken not to frighten the animals, some of which you will certainly see.

The routes selected cover a very wide area of the Exmoor National Park and, in doing so, provide the opportunity to experience the moors and the impressive coastline. The rides are often hilly but when the sun shines the air is crystal clear and fresh. The views are superb and you get a tremendously exhilarating feeling of freedom.

The village of Exford is an ideal centre and base to stay, although there are other equally delightful villages nearby with accommodation and attractions to visit.

This is a truly beautiful place to come mountain biking and if you get tired of wheeling your way across the moorlands, you can always swap your saddle for that of one of the ponies — there are many pony trekking centres throughout Exmoor.

Bike Shop	Ralph Colman Cycles 79 Station Road Taunton Somerset TA1 1PB ☎ 0823 275822

This shop stocks mountain bikes and sells bikes and mountain bike hire.

Places to Stay	Lorna Doone Hotel Porlock Somerset ☎ 0643 862404	Exmoor Lodge Exford Somerset ☎ 0643 83615
	Exmoor House Hotel Exford Somerset TA24 7PY ☎ 0643 83304	Westerclose Country House Hotel Withypool Somerset TA24 7QR ☎ 0643 83302
Places of Interest	*Dunster Castle* near Minehead ☎ 0643 821314	A magnificent thirteenth-century stronghold which rises dramatically above Dunster village and the sea on the edge of Exmoor. There is a 300-year-old staircase and ceiling as well as terraced gardens and shrubs. Open: Easter to September, 11am-5pm, October 2-4pm, daily except Friday and Saturday.

West Somerset Railway
The Railway Station
Minehead
Somerset
TA24 5BG
☎ 0643 704996

Britain's longest independent steam railway. The line is 30km (20 miles) long through the beautiful Somerset hills and coastal scenery from Bishops Lydeard near Taunton to Minehead, the gateway to Exmoor.

Train services March to October, Christmas and the New Year.

Hancocks Devon Cider and Mineral Waters
Clapworthy Mill
South Molton
North Devon
☎ 07695 2678

No visit to this part of the country would be complete without the inevitable visit to a cider makers. Clapworthy Mill offers tours which show the traditional methods of cider production. Also, take a look at the cider presses, the museum corner and the barrels holding the vintage cider. There is also a craft shop with the best from the local craftsmen and local country produce and a full off-licence where you can choose from Hancocks' selection of four local ciders.

Open: the shop is open all year from Monday to Saturday and tours are from Easter to end of October.

Exmoor Bird Gardens
South Stowford
Bratton Fleming
Blackmoor Gate
Devon
☎ 05983 352

This is a tropical bird garden set in 12 acres of the North Devon countryside. The landscaped gardens contain streams, waterfall and lakes with penguins, waterfowl and swans. The aviaries have tropical birds, pheasants and rare breeds of poultry. Small animals can be seen, including wallabies, llama, ponies, monkeys and goats.

Open: April to October 10am-6pm, November to March 10am-4pm.

Tropiquaria
Washford Cross
near Watchet
West Somerset
☎ 0984 40688

Tropiquaria is an indoor tropical jungle containing fascinating plants, free flying birds, iguanas, pythons, toads and terrapins. There is the opportunity to come face to face with a snake and hang one around your neck if you are feeling brave. Also on offer are tropical and local marine fish. There is a garden and picnic area, gift shop, viewing balcony, outdoor aviaries and cafeteria.
Open: every day from 10am.

River Exe and Brendon Hills Ride

56km (35 miles)
Landranger Map 1:50,000 Sheet 181
Starting Point: Exford Map Ref 853 384

Brief Description
A very hilly and difficult ride on lonely moorland lanes and well defined forest tracks on this most scenic region of North-East Exmoor.

The Route
Leave Exford on the B3224 heading east. After 7$\frac{1}{2}$km (4$\frac{1}{2}$ miles) you will come to Wheddon Cross at the junction of the A396. Turn left and immediately right onto a very narrow lane. Take the right fork to the end of the lane and, as it bears left, take the track which continues straight on and drops very sharply into the wooded valley. Crossing over the stream, the stony track climbs very steeply and then levels out towards Couple Cross.

At Couple Cross join a better quality lane which goes straight over towards Luxborough. The lane slopes

24

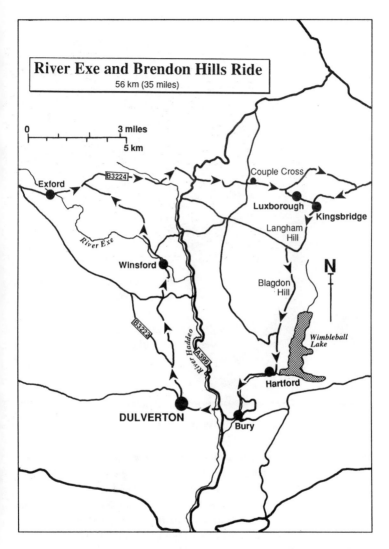

River Exe and Brendon Hills Ride
56 km (35 miles)

0   3 miles

5 km

Exford

B3224

Couple Cross

Luxborough

Kingsbridge

River Exe

Langham
Hill

Winsford

N

Blagdon
Hill

B3224

Wimbleball
Lake

River Haddeo

A396

Hartford

DULVERTON

Bury

downhill to the T-junction where you turn left and immediately right onto a track which leads into the southern
edge of Croydon Hill Forest. Climb for about 2km (1¼

A cautious descent

miles) up to a crossroads of forest and moorland tracks and take the second track on your right that passes through the northern edge of Monkham Hill and descends into moorland and eventually onto a narrow lane. Very careful navigation is called for in this section as there are several forest tracks which could take you right away from the route if your map reading is not up to scratch.

At the lane turn right and descend into Slowley Wood and to Kingsbridge. From Kingsbridge head south and fork right and then left off the lane to join another track which leads to the Brendon Hills. Go through the woodland around Langham Hill. Turn right at the T-junction and left along a narrow lane which goes over Blagdon Hill. Continue southwards now, passing west of Wimbleball Lake for 7km (4$\frac{1}{3}$ miles) to Hartford.

Just before Hartford the lane becomes a rough track and just over the river by the lake this track heads west and follows the line of the River Haddeo through the woodland to Bury. From Bury join a better quality lane which climbs steeply to join the A396 and then the B3222 climbing again to Dulverton. From the village of Dulverton a track which leads from the church proceeds north in the direction of Winsford. This track runs parallel with the B3223 for a few kilometres before joining a lane which climbs to South Hill, drops down, climbs and descends once more to the track which runs by the River Exe in Winsford.

From Winsford follow the lane which heads north-west alongside the river. Where the river bends to the left in 2km (1¼ miles) stay on the lane as it veers right by the side of Larcombe Brook. This lane leads back to the B3224 where you turn left and head back to Exford.

Exmoor Ride

58km (36 miles)
Landranger Map 1:50,000 Sheets 180 and 181
Starting Point: Exford Map Ref 853 384

Brief Description *A very demanding route on bridleways, tracks and good quality narrow lanes over the very beautiful hills and valleys of Exmoor. You will certainly need to be in good condition for this tour.*

The Route Leave Exford on the narrow lane that heads south-east off the B3224 in the direction of Court Farm. After only a short distance the lane turns sharp right and climbs steeply to join the B3223 going south. Turn left and then fork right at the signpost for Withypool. As you ride downhill turn right onto a poorer quality lane/track just before you enter the village of Withypool.

Follow this for 2km (1¼ miles), climbing as you do so until the track becomes a bridleway. Cross over the lane ahead continuing on the bridleway. There are two forks to the right, but keep left and on the main track, which is the Two Moors Way. The track heads down towards the River Barle and through a small plantation. Cross the river by a ford and climb quite steeply to join a stony track by Horsen Farm. Bear left and head for the junction of the lane which leads south from Simonsbath.

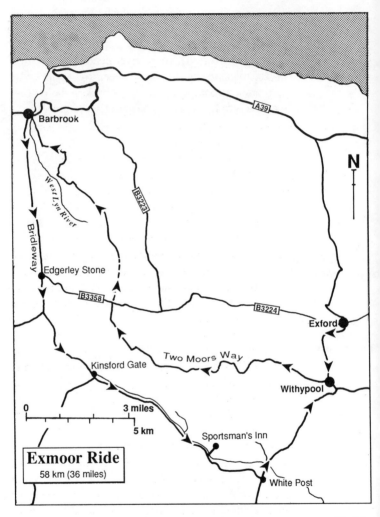

Turn left onto the lane and in a few metres you will pick out the bridleway on the right. It continues as the Two Moors Way going across Exmoor, dropping sharply to cross the River Barle again and climbing very steeply, passing through Cornham Farm to turn left onto the

B3358. After $\frac{1}{2}$km ($\frac{1}{3}$ mile) look out for the Two Moors Way track on the right and follow this very hilly and beautiful section for a further 7km ($4\frac{1}{2}$ miles) heading north until the bridleway joins a stony track at Stock Common. Head left there and join the narrow lane which drops down into Barbrook.

It is well worth taking a good rest in Barbrook because there is no relenting in the route as you head back onto Exmoor for the return section.

Turn left onto the A39 in Barbrook and immediately left again over the West Lyn River, climbing very steeply up the narrow lane which heads south over the western edge of Exmoor. The lane deteriorates gradually as you climb and eventually becomes a bridleway by Saddle Gate. Continue the ascent for another 2km ($1\frac{1}{4}$ miles) until you reach a high point at Wood Barrow. There are some fine views to be enjoyed at this point towards the coast, to the south and around the moors. Descend south to cross over the B3358 following the bridleway in a southerly direction for 2km ($1\frac{1}{4}$ miles) to join a narrow lane by a sharp bend.

Follow this lane south, climbing yet again to the crossroads of Kinsford Gate. Go straight over to a high point around Hangley Cleave and once again take time to enjoy the superb views across Exmoor. The cycling becomes easier at last as the lane drops gradually towards the Sportsman's Inn at the next junction. Turn right and immediately left, then left at the next crossroads along narrow lanes until you come to the White Post crossroads. Take the track which heads north from there crossing Litton Water. Continue along the track which becomes another bridleway after 2km ($1\frac{1}{4}$ miles) and follow this to join the lane into Withypool. From there head north retracing the route back to Exford.

Somerset and North Devon Coastal Ride

52km (32 miles)
Landranger Map 1:50,000 Sheets 180 and 181
Starting Point: Exford Map Ref 853 384

Brief Description *A very strenuous but extremely beautiful ride along well defined bridleways, forest tracks and good quality country lanes over the Northern Exmoor hills and coastal path.*

The Route Leave Exford on the narrow lane which climbs steeply heading north from the B3224 towards Hillhead Cross. Just where a lane forks to the right, a track/bridleway goes left to Almsworthy Common. After about 3km (2 miles) cross over the lane by a cattle grid following the bridle-path in a north-west direction over the moors for 8km (5 miles) until you drop down into the village of Oare. Turn left by the church and right onto a lane which crosses over Oare Water. Continue up the hillside to join the A39 and turn right along the main road for $2^1/_2$km ($1^1/_2$ miles) until you come to a track on the left known as the Somerset and North Devon Coast Path.

This track descends quite steeply towards the sea and then heads east passing Silcombe Farm, Ash Farm and Yarner Farm towards Porlock. Once you are past the last farm there is a choice of two routes you can take. One heads left from the valley onto a narrow lane in the direction of the coast to join the B3225 and the other is a woodland track which passes through Worthy Wood, joins a lane and heads into Porlock.

Join the A39 in Porlock and continue along this for 3km (2 miles) to the tiny village of Holnicote. Take the lane which heads left signposted to Selworthy. A bridleway located by the church heads north through the woodland

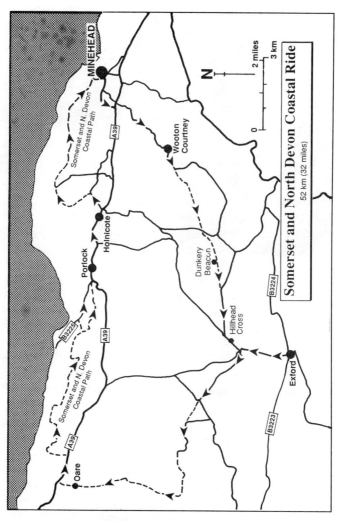

Somerset and North Devon Coastal Ride

52 km (32 miles)

passing Bury Castle. Climbing out of the trees, you can follow the track right or left to join the Somerset and North Devon Coast Path. Head east along this, enjoying the lovely views over the sea as you do so, and into Minehead.

The pretty village of Allerford, near Porlock

In Minehead work your way to the A39. By the caravan site in Bratton there is a sharp bend in the road and a lane which heads off to the right. Go along this lane for $\frac{1}{2}$km ($\frac{1}{3}$mile), after which a stony track climbs steeply through the forest known as Great Headon Plantation and eventually descends into Wooton Courtney. Very careful navigation is needed if you are to attempt this section through the forest. You can either head to Dunster from Minehead, following the Wooton sign from the A396, or cycle west from Minehead on the A39 and follow the sign for Tivington and Wooton.

From Wooton Courtney a narrow farm track heads left past the post office. Follow this until it joins a bridleway which climbs very steeply for a long 4km ($2\frac{1}{2}$ miles) to Dunkery Beacon. This is a most strenuous climb but the views from the summit make the effort well worthwhile. Continue along the summit ridge heading west to join the lane that takes you down to Hillhead Cross and drops steeply back into Exford.

Chapter 3

The South Downs

As you head further south and east in England the possibilities for good mountain biking trips tend to become much reduced. After the rugged moorlands and high plateaux of central and northern England, Wales and Scotland anything else seems relatively flat and undemanding. However, in the south-east of England, and just inland from the chalk cliffs of the South Coast, the chalk ridges and the green rolling hills of the South Downs provide one of the last challenges and two very enjoyable rides on and around these hills can be recommended.

The South Downs Way is an obvious attraction and one of the rides follows a section of this popular track in some really fine countryside. There are several tracks and narrow lanes which criss-cross the Downs, thereby making them a very easy place to explore. This region is not as wild as areas in the north of the country but it is certainly very pretty and at various points along the Downs Way you are rewarded with views looking out to sea.

The towns of Arundel and Petworth are ideal locations to be based for these rides. Petworth lies just to the north-east of the South Downs on the junction of the A283 and A285 above the River Rother. The beautiful deer park is sited to the west of the A283 and is the starting point for one of the rides.

Arundel, some 18km (11 miles) south of Petworth, is set in a very attractive location on the eastern edge of the Downs on the junction of the A27 and the A284 about 7km ($4^1/_3$ miles) from the South Coast resort of Littlehampton. The River Arun winds its way through the edge of the town and flows out to sea. When you are not biking it is a great place to explore. Arundel Park, with its lake and nearby wildfowl reserve, is well worth spending some time in, as is the castle. Country parks appear to be among the main features of the South Downs; they certainly add to what is already a very attractive region.

Bike Shop
Rowes
The Hornet
Chichester
PO19 4JW
☎ 0243 788100

Places to Stay

Bridge House and Cottage
18 Queen Street
Arundel
☎ 0903 882142

Offham House
Offham
near Arundel
☎ 0903 882122

Arundel House Guest House
11 High Street
Arundel
☎ 0903 882136

Eastwood Farm
Graffham
Petworth
☎ 07986 317

Places of Interest

Arundel Castle
Arundel
West Sussex
☎ 0903 883136

This is the ancestral home of the Dukes of Norfolk. It is a well restored Norman stronghold which stands on a mound beside the River Arun. There is an eleventh-century keep and thirteenth-century barbican, barons' hall, armoury chapel, library and gallery. During the Arundel Festival in August, the castle's American Ground is the stage for open-air theatre. There is also a gift shop and tea garden. Open: May to end September. Times vary, phone for details. Not open on event days.

Goodwood House
Goodwood
near Chichester
West Sussex
☎ 0243 774107

Set in a large area of open parkland, this magnificent eighteenth-century house is the home of the Dukes of Richmond and Gordon. The house is furnished with tapestries, French furniture, porcelain and a major collection of paintings. Being closely linked with the 'Glorious Goodwood Racecourse' and horses, important

34

equestrian events take place at the International Dressage Centre in the park. There is also a golf course, airfield and motor circuit. Open: mid-April to early October, generally 2-5pm.

Petworth House
and Country
Park
Petworth
West Sussex
☎ 0798 42207

This is a late seventeenth-century house which is sited in a large deer park. It was designed by 'Capability' Brown and painted by Turner whose paintings are included in the house's private collection. Noted for its carvings by Grinling Gibbons, there are also collections of furniture by the Third Earl of Egremont.
Open: mid-April to early October, Wednesday, Thursday, Sunday and Bank Holiday Mondays 2-6pm.

West Dean Gardens
West Dean
near Chichester
West Sussex
☎ 024363 303

Established in the early seventeenth century, the present West Dean Gardens were enlarged when the house (now a crafts college) was built in the early nineteenth century. Included in the 35 acres of gardens are some massive old specimen trees. There is also a pergola draped with roses, rustic summer houses and a wild garden. Victorian greenhouses contain a large collection of lawnmowers and an exhibition on the garden's history.
Open: March to October daily 10am-6pm.

The Wildfowl
and Wetlands
Centre
Mill Road
Arundel
West Sussex
☎ 0903 883355

The wildfowl trust's reserve has an observatory and hides covering 55 acres of water meadow beside the River Arun. There is a large variety of tame swans, ducks and geese and other birds from around the world, including some rare and endangered species. A visitor centre provides a viewing gallery, film theatre and gift shop.
Open: all year, daily, generally from 9.30am-5.30pm.

South Downs Ride 1

43km (27 miles); 50km (31 miles) with extensions round
Iodsworth and Leggatt Hill
Landranger Map 1:50,000 Sheet 197
Starting Point: Petworth Map Ref 967 216

**Brief
Description**

*An easy ride on good quality narrow country lanes, a few
bridlepaths through some really lovely countryside and
villages of southern England.*

The Route

This ride starts at the south-east corner of Petworth Park.
Just before Petworth House a well defined track leads off
the A285 and heads right through the park, passing the
lake, and towards the woodland at the top section of the
park. Follow the track into the woodland, known as
Pheasant Copse. Avoid the tracks that join the main route
through the park, continue past Stagpark Farm and head
for another plantation where, upon entering, you take the
left of the two forks to join the lane at Old Mill Farm.

Follow the narrow lane straight across from Mill Farm
and after a short distance go right to Lurgashall and then
left by the pub to Dial Green. These are very tiny places
indeed with only a few houses and a minimum of facilities. At Dial Green turn right and immediately to your
left is a stony track which leads to Great Brockhurst Farm
and a bridleway that heads across the countryside and
joins a lane after $1^1/_2$km (1 mile). Follow this lane and take
the first right turn to Fernhurst.

Take the lane which goes past the church and crosses
the A286 to Elmers Marsh. Turn left at the T-junction and
stay on this lane for Milland. Go over the crossroads at
Milland following the sign for Hill Brow. The lane climbs
gradually into the woodland as you head towards Hill
Brow. About 2km ($1^1/_4$ miles) from the A3 turn left at the
crossroads, following the signpost to Rogate. Continue
through the wooded lane downhill for 1km ($^2/_3$ mile)

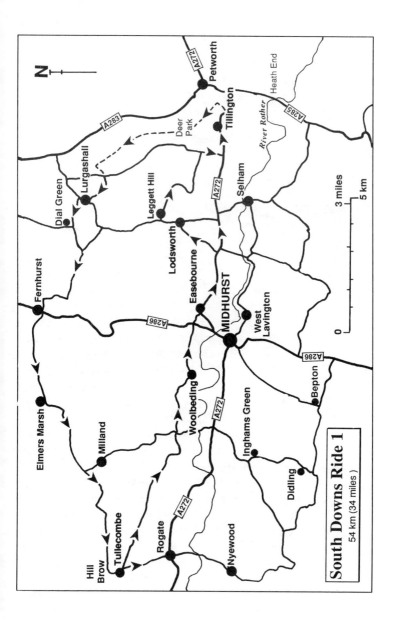

South Downs Ride 1
54 km (34 miles)

Enjoying the fresh air and sunshine

turning first left in the tiny village of Tullecombe. This narrow wooded lane now gives pleasant riding, descending for 3km (2 miles). Where the lane bears right at the next crossroads join the track that continues through the edge of the wood and eventually rejoining a lane to pass by the southern edge of Hammer Wood.

At the next junction turn left. Quiet country lanes with good surfaces are followed to the village of Woolbeding. Turn left towards Easebourne. Cross over the A286 in Easebourne onto a lane which joins the A272. Pass the church and after a further $2^1/_2$km ($1^1/_2$ miles) a narrow lane on the left leads through the woodland to Lodsworth. This is an optional deviation on the route. If your legs are feeling tired at this point then the most obvious way is to stay on the A272 all the way to Petworth. However the route is far more interesting and certainly quieter along the fairly tame hills through to Lodsworth and beyond. Turning left at any of the lanes in the village continue to the triangle and head right at Leggatt Hill. Follow this winding narrow lane in the direction of Petworth Park. You have the option of joining the A272 at any of three lanes which lead off this deviation, riding into the village of Tillington. Stay on the main road back to Petworth.

South Downs Ride 2

54km (34 miles)
Landranger Map 1:50,000 Sheet 197
Starting Point: Arundel Map Ref 013 069

Brief Description *A route of medium difficulty on mostly well defined bridleways and good quality country lanes over the moors, beautiful woodlands and parks of the South Downs. Good map skills are called for throughout this ride.*

The Route From the roundabout in the centre of Arundel follow the A284 north for about 1km ($^2/_3$ mile) until a lane on the right leads to the southern entrance of Arundel Park. As you enter into the park, ride along the track that goes past the tower and runs parallel with the A284 to Whiteways Lodge by the next major roundabout. Take the A29 north off the roundabout and immediately there is a bridleway which heads left through Houghton Forest. Follow this and climb towards the edge of the forest for 2km ($1^1/_4$ miles) until you come to a crossroads. Turn right on that bridleway known as the Denture and keep riding up to the car park.

You will pass a Neolithic camp just before the car park. You then go over a Roman road across Burton Down and descend to Littleton Farm on the A285. There are several tracks in the area between Whiteways Lodge and the A285 and accurate map reading is called for if you intend to stay on the proposed route.

Cross the A285 to join another bridleway. This is the South Downs Way, the first 6km ($3^3/_4$ miles) being all uphill through woodland. Several tracks either cross or join this bridleway, avoid them and continue in a westerly direction descending 3km (nearly 2 miles) to the A286, leaving the woodland as you descend. Cross the A-road and continue on the South Downs Way climbing quite

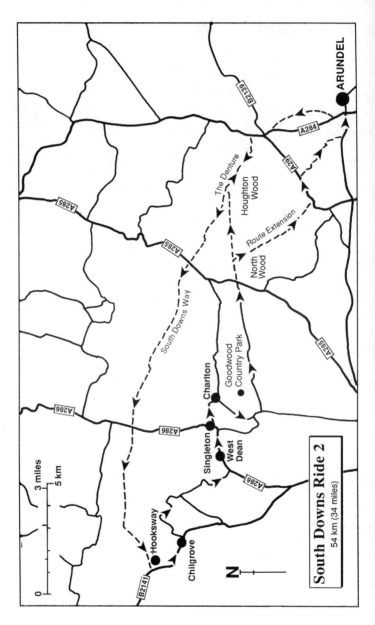

South Downs Ride 2

54 km (34 miles)

steeply; the route runs in between the trees here. After about 3km (nearly 2 miles) you begin to drop down again and follow the South Downs Way as it bares left to Hooksway.

Carry on to the B2141, turning left to Chilgrove. Just around the bend at Chilgrove, follow the narrow lane that heads left to West Dean. Go over the crossroads, climb up the farm track and drop down into West Dean and the A286. Turning left on the main road, follow it round past the Weald and Downland Open Air Museum to Singleton and take the narrow lane signposted Charlton. In Charlton you can take either of the two lanes on the right that lead to Goodwood Country Park. Although a place to avoid on race days, it is a lovely park and there are plenty of parking and picnic places available.

Follow the lane which heads east out of Goodwood Park to Selhurst Park and the junction of the A285. From that point there is a vast choice of routes back to Arundel. One obvious route is to follow the bridleway opposite the lane, retracing your tracks along the Denture to Whiteways and Arundel. You can follow the same track from the lane and turn right after 1km ($^2/_3$ mile) to Northwood and, again, you can take any suitable track back to base. Alternatively, if you do not feel up to some good, accurate navigation, turn right at the lane onto the A285. Turn left after $1^1/_2$km (1 mile) along a narrow lane to Slindon via Eartham and the A27 back to Arundel.

Chapter 4

Peak District
and Sherwood Forest

These two regions of central England have been selected for one of the areas covered in the book due to their close proximity to each other and their contrasting scenery.

The Peak District National Park which covers 330km² (540sq miles) contains some of the most picturesque moorland countryside in Britain. The southern half of the Peak District is dissected by green gorges, limestone cliffs and wooded valleys whose rivers often start their course somewhere in the Northern Peak. Further north the Rivers Noe, Derwent and the Goyt have carved wider and flatter valleys and to the far north of the region the Kinder Scout and Bleaklow Plateaux are areas of wild moorland with wet, inhospitable peat bogs.

Undoubtedly the best areas considered suitable for mountain biking exist in the central, southern and western parts of the Peak District. These regions provide a wide range of typical Peak District scenery as well as good quality country lanes and bridleways. Clearly the routes are often hilly and some sections quite difficult, but the views, for the most part, are well worth any strenuous biking.

In Sherwood Forest, an area that has seen an influx of tourist activity in recent years with various craft centres and holiday parks, the region lends itself to several tracks of varying quality. By comparison with the hills of the Peak District, this area is mostly flat and the cycling easy. You will, however, need good map reading skills to follow some of the many tracks available.

Because the rides in this area stretch far and wide, the towns of

Bakewell, Buxton and in Sherwood Forest the villages of Edwinstowe and Ollerton are the most suitably situated places in which to be based.

Bakewell is a small market town sited on the banks of the River Wye on the A6 and the junction of the A619, 18km (11 miles) east of Buxton. It is very much a tourist centre with many attractions, including a medieval bridge over the Wye and a colourful and lively market on Mondays.

Buxton lies at the head of the Wye and is one of the highest towns in England. It is renowned for the medicinal qualities of its waters. The Romans laid the foundations of what has developed into one of England's most popular inland spas.

The Peak District, like other national parks in Britain, is very sensitive to over-use. When you look on a map there seems to be a wide choice of places to go. Indeed, the many footpaths make most areas readily accessible, but this is not the case with mountain biking. Although you can share a few routes with walkers, most of which are on bridleways, it is these and other similar tracks and the narrow moorland country lanes which must be used to avoid conflict with other users of the countryside and to stay within the law.

Bike Shops

Cyclone
76 Bridge Street
Belper
Derbyshire
DE5 1AZ
☎ 0773 821428

This shop sells mountain bikes, equipment and accessories. Repairs are also carried out. The owner is a keen mountain biker and a warm welcome and advice are always given.

Rex Robinson Cycles
27 Burton Road
Carlton
Nottingham
NG4 3DT
☎ 0602 619069

Places to Stay

Sherwood Forest

Forest Lodge Hotel
2 Church Street
Edwinstowe
NG21 9QA
☎ 0623 822970

Friars Lodge Guest House
3 Mill Lane
Edwinstowe
NG21 9QY
☎ 0623 823405

Ollerton House Hotel
Wellow Road
Ollerton
NG22 9AP
☎ 0623 861017

Bakewell

The Lathkill Hotel
Over Haddon
near Bakewell
Derbyshire
DE4 1JE
☎ 062981 2501

Castle Cliff Hotel
Monsal Head
Great Longstone
DE4 1NL
☎ 062987 258

Buxton

Buxton Lodge Guest House
28 London Road
Buxton
SK17 9NX
☎ 0298 3522

Griff Guest House
2 Compton Road
Buxton
☎ 0298 3628

Places of Interest

Chatsworth House
Chatsworth
near Bakewell
☎ 024688 2204

Situated in a beautiful park and woodland, the seventeenth-century palace of Chatsworth House is home to the Duke and Duchess of Devonshire. It contains one of the richest collections of fine and decorative art in private hands. Numerous events are held throughout the year. There is a farming and forestry exhibition and guided tours are also on offer by prior arrangement. House and gardens are open daily from late March to October.

Old House Museum
Cunningham Place
off Church Lane
Bakewell
☎ 062981 3647

This is an early Tudor house with original wattle and daub interior walls and an open timbered chamber. There is an exhibition of costumes, Victorian kitchen, farming equipment, toys, lacework and craftsmens tools. Open: late March to October 2-5pm daily.

Chatsworth House and its grounds

Pooles Cavern
Buxton Country
 Park
Green Lane
Buxton
☎ 0298 6978

Pooles Cavern is a natural limestone cavern in 100 acres of woodland. It includes a visitor centre with video show and exhibition of cave and woodland including archaeology finds from the cave dig. Open: Good Friday to end October daily 10am-5pm.

As you head east from Buxton towards Castleton you can take guided tours around the famous Blue John Mines which venture deep into the surrounding Derbyshire hills. Another tour is conducted by boat on the underground canals of Speedwell Cavern, while Peak Cavern is an impressive natural cave. Blue John souvenirs are on sale at the small shops by the entrance to the caves and in the gift shops of Castleton.

Rufford Abbey
Rufford Country
 Park
Ollerton
Near Newark
Nottinghamshire
☎ 0623 824153

Rufford Abbey is located in the very attractive woodland and parkland of Rufford Country Park which has a beautiful lake with many species of waterfowl and a meadow with rare species of sheep. The abbey dates back to 1170 and was originally used by monks until 1536. After that time it was used as a hunting lodge by George Talbot, Fourth Earl of Shrewsbury. Today, the stable is used as an extensive craft centre and boasts a fine selection of hand worked crafts such as jewellery, glass and pottery. It also contains a gallery which features a programme of major craft exhibitions each year. The coach house is used as a café and provides a variety of snacks and beverages.

Contact the rangers on the number provided for details of tours.

Open: daily Easter to end September 10am-5pm; daily October to Easter 10am-4pm.

Clumber Park
Worksop
Nottinghamshire
☎ 0909 476592

Sited in the northern part of Sherwood Forest, Clumber Park offers 3,800 acres of parkland and woodlands as well as Clumber Chapel. It was formerly the home park of the Nottinghamshire estates of the Dukes of Newcastle. It now belongs to the National Trust and is open to the public at all times. There are local maps and guides available which detail the park's rich and varied bird and wild life.

Sherwood Forest
  Visitor Centre and
  Country Park
Edwinstowe
near Mansfield
Nottinghamshire
☎ 0623 823202

This is the magnificent woodland of Sherwood Forest, once homeland to the world's most famous outlaw, Robin Hood. Many tracks lead through the woodlands including the one to Robin Hood's favourite hideout, The Major Oak. The visitor centre houses Robin Hood relics and memorabilia. There is a wide range of events and literature based on the outlaw's life. Souvenirs and gifts are available and a tourist information centre to help with all your needs. Robin Hood's Larder provides light meals and snacks with a unique Robin Hood theme.

The park and visitor centre are open all year. Robin Hood's Larder opens at various times throughout the year so it may be worth checking on those times before your planned visit.

Church Farm Craft
Workshops
Mansfield Road
Edwinstowe
Nottinghamshire
NG21 9NJ
☎ 0623 823767

Housed in traditionally restored former farmhouse out-buildings, the farm craft workshops offer the visitor the opportunity to view the craftspeople at their work. A wide range of crafts, from steam engines to furniture restoring, are constantly being worked at, the exhibits of which are generally on sale to the public.

Open throughout the year, Thursday to Sunday and bank holidays approximately 10am-5pm. Some workshops are open all week.

Western Peak District Ride

62km (38 miles)
Landranger Map 1:50,000 Sheets 118 and 119
Starting Point: Horwich End near Whaley Bridge Map
Ref 010 806

Brief
Description
This is a truly spectacular ride. For much of the route you are rewarded with some outstanding Peak District scenery. To be fully enjoyed it is well worth stretching the ride out over two days. There are some easy sections and some strenuous hill climbs on mostly good quality lanes over the high Staffordshire moorlands.

The Route
From Horwich End follow the B5089 that leads from the crossroads of the A6 and the A625. After 1km ($^2/_3$ mile) you come to a narrow lane where you head left. Continue along this lane past the junction as far as it goes to join the track which leads into the Dale of Goyt. Ride for 5km (3 miles) passing Fernilee Reservoir. This track then leads onto a narrow stony lane by Errwood Reservoir and then proceeds in a southerly direction crossing Goyts Moss, passing Derbyshire Bridge until coming to a T-junction.

Turn right and immediately left, crossing over the A537 and A54 in quick succession to ride along the lane which goes over Axe Edge Moor for 2km ($1^1/_4$ miles). Go over the crossroads of the A53 and join the lane which drops past Leap Edge until you come to a junction at Thirkelow. Turn right there and follow this narrow lane which passes Chrome Hill and Hollins Hill and join the B5053. Turn right to Longnor. Just past the church in Longnor take the left turn heading towards Sheen and, about $^1/_2$km ($^1/_3$ mile) along the lane, turn left again, dropping down to cross over the River Dove, climbing out of Crowdicote to the crossroads at High Needham. Turn right there and continue past the next crossroads heading south; just past Vincent House take the right fork

48

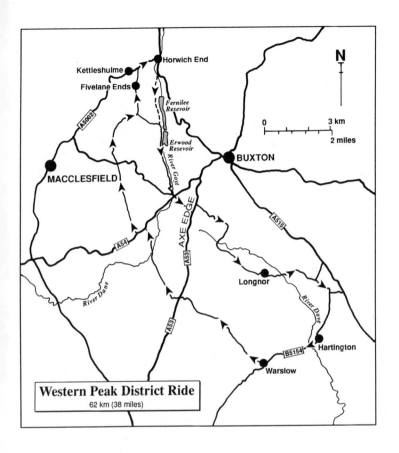

Western Peak District Ride
62 km (38 miles)

that leads to Hartington.

In Hartington, a very popular village with tourists in the summer months, turn right onto the B5054 signposted to Warslow. At the T-junction in 4km (2¹/₂ miles) turn left onto the B5053 into Warslow village and take the right turn just before the church along the lane signposted to Newtown and Leek. Pass the Greyhound Inn on the right and continue up the lane. It eventually evens out and you are soon riding in some really wild moorland.

Where the sign points to Leek fork right. Go over the

crossroads ahead and make for the hill in the distance and the road that climbs up its centre. Ride downhill to a small plantation turning sharp right at the bridge. Just past here take the left fork and continue up the hill previously sighted. As you approach the panorama includes the imposing gritstone edges of the Roaches to the west. As you come to the next junction follow the road to Royal Cottage. This will take you to the A53. Cross over to join the lane marker Allgreave and Gradbach. At first there is quite a fast slope to descend and in a short distance the lane heads to the right. Continue along this fast and twisting lane for 3km (2 miles). Towards the end you drop to a T-junction facing a stone cottage. Go left here and cross over the River Dane. Climb the hill for a short distance before taking the road that angles sharp right through a metal gate. This introduces you to a very steep climb on a narrow moorland track. Great care is needed along this stretch which at times is very strenuous. Three more gates are encountered along the track.

Turn left at the end of this lane onto the A54 and after 1km take the lane on the right signposted Wildboar-clough. This beautiful section which by the side of a pine wood. You soon leave the trees behind though. Keep right at the 'Macc Forest' sign. A single track road provides excellent biking with Macclesfield Forest to the left. Pass two Forest Chapel signs. Turn left at the T-junction by the Stanley Arms and climb the long hill to the A537.

Cross over and descend the very steep and winding lane marked Goyt Valley. After 3km (2miles) you come to a triangle where you head right, again following the Goyt Valley sign. At the bottom of this slope you are then faced with another low-gear situation where all your energy is required for one last climb. Continue to Jenkin Chapel and turn right uphill to Pym Chair at the top of the ridge. Go left here and enjoy the stunning views as you pedal freely downhill to the A5002. Turn right on the A-road as you head back to Whaley Bridge.

Central Peak District Ride

47km (29 miles)
Landranger Map 1:50,000 Sheet 119
Starting Point Bakewell: Map Ref 216 685

Brief Description

A much varied route on good quality lanes and well defined tracks over moorland and Derbyshire dales. A moderately difficult ride.

The Route

Leave Bakewell on the A619 signposted to Sheffield. Cross the bridge over the River Wye and turn immediately right, going up Castle Hill and heading towards the north-west corner of Manners Wood. Bear sharp right and, about half way down the road, descend the narrow lane into Edensor. The track surface improves considerably over the last 200m. Pass through this delightful village with St Peter's church to the right. Go over the cattle grid, through the white gates to join the B6012.

For those wishing to spend some time in or around Chatsworth House turn right along the B-road and follow the entrance signs to the left. The road goes over the River Derwent and into the parking area by the side of the house. Several tracks which take on the appearance of ideal mountain bike paths lead into the woodlands behind the house. Unfortunately these are concessionary paths only — no bikes are allowed.

After a visit to Chatsworth rejoin the B6012 and head north out of the park until you reach the A619 just south of Baslow.

Head right on the main road and carry on past the roundabout to the Robin Hood Inn. Take the B6050 left for 2¹/₂km (1¹/₂ miles) to Bleak House. At the crossroads head left along the narrow lane for 3km (nearly 2 miles) crossing the A621. In a few metres on the other side of the main road follow the grassy track on the other side of the turnstile and gate that leads to Wellington's Monument.

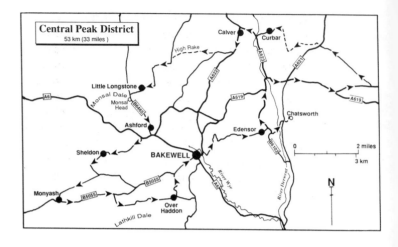

On reaching the monument, head right along the top of Baslow Edge until you come to a lane where you turn left and drop down into Curbar.

When the going gets tough . . . .

Join the A623 turning right and, crossing over the River Derwent, go into Calver. Climb out of the limestone village on the B6001 in the direction of Bakewell. After 1km (²/₃ mile) a stony track on the right opposite the junction of a narrow lane will take you quite steeply uphill and to High Rake. You pass old mines and quarries on the track and continue until you reach the bend of a narrow lane. Turn left at the bend and descend towards a T-junction where you go right to Monsal Head. It is well worth taking a look at the old railway viaduct and to perhaps walk your bike down alongside the river to view the weir.

Ride down the B6465 to Ash-

52

ford and you will come out on the A6. Turn right and first left along a narrow lane signposted to Sheldon and Monyash. You can either go to Sheldon or carry on along Kirk Dale and take the second right to Monyash. Turn left onto the B5055, and staying on this road, pass the turn off for Lathkill Dale. Unfortunately, cycling is not allowed along this beautiful valley, so continue to the next junction on the right and follow the narrow road which runs parallel with and overlooks the dale. Go through Over Haddon and take the left-hand lane which leads off a bend to rejoin the B5055. Turn right and head back to Bakewell.

Sherwood Forest Ride

44km (27 miles)
Landranger map 1:50,000 Sheet 120
Starting Point: Apleyhead Lodge off A614 and A57 Map Ref 645 774

Brief Description

An easy ride over good quality lanes and tracks through Sherwood Forest. This is not a particularly long route, thereby providing the time needed to have a good look around the country parks and craft centres.

The Route

You can park anywhere there is a suitable gap along the narrow wooded lane that leads from Apleyhead Lodge or you can drive into Clumber Park and use the car park there (parking fee payable).

You are really spoilt for choice of routes in Sherwood Forest as there are numerous extensions you can take and ride along at your own pace. The route selected here is one that gives the opportunity to visit the various visitor amenities and covers the main area of this enormous forest.

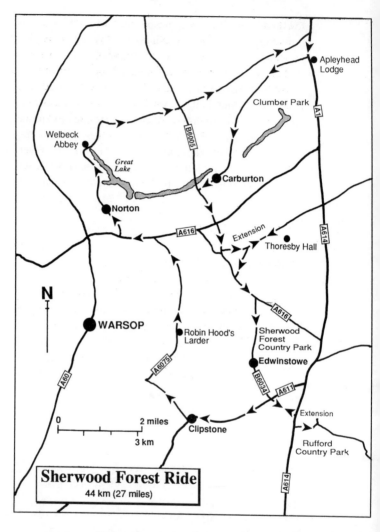

Apleyhead
Lodge

Clumber Park

Welbeck
Abbey

*Great
Lake*

B6005

Carburton

Norton

A1

A616

A614

Extension

Thoresby Hall

N

WARSOP

Robin Hood's
Larder

Sherwood
Forest
Country Park

A616

A60

A6075

Edwinstowe

B6034

A611

Extension

0   2 miles

3 km

Clipstone

Rufford
Country Park

A614

Sherwood Forest Ride

44 km (27 miles)

If you are starting from Apleyhead Lodge, follow the narrow lane towards Carburton, taking any of three extensions into Clumber Park. At Carburton cross over the bridge and continue along the lane to join the B6005. Turn left and after 2km ($1\frac{1}{4}$ miles) you will come to a cross-roads with a narrow lane and the A616. This is called Fanny's Grove and you can turn left here to ride to Thoresby Hall and Lake. Coming back along this lane, take the track which heads left by Cameleon Lodge and pass the western edge of the lake to join the A616. Turn left on the main road and ride for $1\frac{1}{2}$km (1 mile) to join the B6034 which will take you into Edwinstowe and Sherwood Forest Country Park.

Carry on along the B-road heading towards Rufford Country Park and Rufford Abbey. There are craft workshops in Edwinstowe and a craft and visitor centre at Rufford where exhibitions are frequently held. From Rufford, backtrack along the B6034 to the crossroads of the B6030 and turn left for Clipstone. At Clipstone, and virtually opposite King Johns Palace, take the narrow lane that heads right towards Warsop. Go over the railway and, shortly before the junction with the A6075, take the narrow lane on the right. Cross over the A-road and onto the forest track that leads to Robin Hood's Larder. You can also visit the tree centre just to the right of this.

The track goes north past Hanger Hill to join the A616. You can either follow the main road and join the B-road into Norton or continue along one of the forest tracks that leads onto a lane and into the tiny village. From there a well defined track leads through Welbeck Park to Welbeck Abbey. Cross the bridge over the lake opposite the abbey, taking the left fork head towards Welbeck House and in the direction of the B6005. Cross over the road leading to Truman's Lodge. Again, from that vicinity there are several alternatives that lead back to your starting point.

Chapter 5

Yorkshire Dales

The Yorkshire Dales undoubtedly provide some of the finest country-side in Eng'.and. Perhaps the most notable features of this national park are the limestone scenery, the caves, crags, dry stone walls and centuries-old limestone villages, not to mention the sweeping moors and valleys, rivers and waterfalls. The area is already immensely popular with walkers, climbers and tourists but there is also room and ample potential for some rugged mountain bike rides.

The villages of Grassington, Malham and Hawes make ideal centres for the rides in this region, not only for biking but as places of wide-ranging interest to visit and explore.

The giant, curve-shaped limestone cliff at Malham Cove forms a magnificent amphitheatre, rising dramatically to 100m (330ft) and extending more than 300m (1,000ft) in width. Nearby is Malham Tarn, a small lake with attractive waterside walks. The tarn is the highest freshwater lake of its size in England.

Wensleydale and Swaledale are the best known of all the Dales. Swaledale is bounded on either side by steep sided fells and limestone outcrops — the region is certainly very dramatic. On grey days, when the mist is swirling around and the fine drizzle soaks you through, it can be the last place you could wish to be. However, on warm sunny days there are few places to rival the Yorkshire Dales.

The River Ure flows through the length of Wensleydale, dropping down a series of impressive waterfalls. Hardraw Force is the highest waterfall in England, dropping over 30m (100ft). Aysgarth Falls, further down the dale, is a series of smaller waterfalls, leading along a woodland nature trail to a spectacular view of the river. Not far away is one of the Wensleydale landmarks; Bolton Castle, where Mary, Queen of Scots was imprisoned for 6 months by Queen Elizabeth I in 1568.

Askrigg, 11km (7 miles) up the dale is another place where it seems that life has stood still. If it seems that you are standing on the set of a period drama then this is because the fictional BBC series *All Creatures Great and Small* is filmed here. James Herriot fans soon spot Skeldale House, the vets' surgery. In real life, it is an old peoples' home.

Hawes is one of the highest market towns in England, with the Pennine Way running through the centre. It is a good place to shop for specialities of the area, particularly the local cheese, Wensleydale's most famous product. The Tuesday market is a regular meeting place for the two hundred sheep and dairy farmers in the dale and is now a tourist attraction in its own right. The rope works at Hawes are the starting point of the Dales Country Workshop Trail, a route taking in ten traditional crafts, including candle making in Wensley.

Bike Shop

Pletts Barn Mountain
  Bikes
The Mountaineer Ltd
Pletts Barn
Garrs Lane
Grassington
Skipton
North Yorkshire
BD23 5AT
☎ 0756 752266

Bike hire (half day, full day or weekly hire). Maps available. Waterproofs for hire.

Places to Stay

Foresters Arms
Main Street
Grassington
Skipton
North Yorkshire
☎ 0756 752349

Buck Inn
Malham
North Yorkshire
☎ 07293 317

Tennant Arms Hotel
Kilnsey
near Grassington
North Yorkshire
☎ 0756 752301

Rose and Crown Hotel
Bainbridge
Wensleydale
North Yorkshire
☎ 0969 50225

The Cove Centre
Malham
☎ 07293 432

About 100 years ago the Cove Centre was converted from farm buildings into a woollen weaving mill. Despite having a very high reputation in the quality of its woollen cloth, with sales to Saville Row stores and to Royalty, a shortage of skilled craftsmen led to the decline in production. In 1984 the old weaving mill was restored and became known as the Cove Centre. This heralded a return to more traditional crafts such as outdoor clothing and furniture. The centre has built up a reputation for its high quality crafts and now certainly provides a most interesting place to visit in the Dales.

Open: March to November, every day; January to February, weekends only.

Bolton Castle
Wensleydale
☎ 0969 23981

Located just outside the village of Redmire, the castle was built in the fourteenth century by Richard le Scrope (Lord Chancellor of England to Richard II). It is a fascinating medieval castle with halls, chambers, passages and staircases. Partly furnished with much of interest, from dungeon to bedrooms.

Open: daily March to mid November 10am-5pm.

Dales Countryside Museum
Hawes
☎ 0969 667450

Located at Station Yard off the A684 on the Leyburn side of Hawes, this fairly new attraction has been formed by merging the Upper Dales Folk Museum and its collection of bygones of traditional Dales life, with the adjacent national park centre. It explains how the people of the Dales have influenced the evolution of one of Britain's most distinctive landscapes. Exhibits include upland farming, wool and hand knitting, stone cutting, lead mining, dairying and cheese making.

Open: daily April to October 10am-5pm, some winter weekend opening.

Kilnsey Park
Kilnsey
near Skipton
☎ 0756 752150

Attractions include Daleslife Visitor
Centre, trout farm, farm shop, fishing,
refreshments and picnic area.

Wharfedale and Langstrothdale Chase Ride

54km (34 miles)
Landranger Map 1:50,000 Sheet 98
Starting Point: Conistone Map Ref 981 675

Brief Desription

Quite a difficult ride along steep and mostly narrow lanes.

The Route

The car park at Conistone, 5km (3 miles) north of Grassington, provides an ideal starting point for this ride. Cross over the River Wharfe and turn right onto the B6160. The most obvious landmark here is the overwhelming face of Kilnsey Crag. A most daunting and challenging overhanging limestone crag which attracts only the best rock climbers.

Continue north, crossing the River Skirfare, to Kettlewell going back over the Wharfe and on to Starbotton and Buckden. From Buckden a narrow lane veers left, crossing the Wharfe yet again to lead through the steep valley of Langstrothdale, along Dalesway, climbing slowly until you come to Beckermonds.

At Beckermonds the route goes right and be prepared for a very steep ascent lasting about 4km ($2^1/_2$ miles). This brings you to a plateau and the chance to take a well earned breather and to sample the beautiful surrounding moorland and dales. The track goes sharp left and immediately right to join a Roman road climbing even further towards Wether Fell. You then descend quite

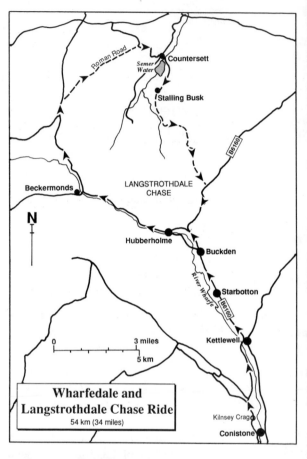

Roman Road

Semer Water

Countersett

Stalling Busk

B6160

LANGSTROTHDALE CHASE

Beckermonds

N

Hubberholme

Buckden

River Wharfe

Starbotton

B6160

0   3 miles

5 km

Kettlewell

**Wharfedale and
Langstrothdale Chase Ride**

54 km (34 miles)

Kilnsey Crag

Conistone

sharply after Wether Fell for about 3km (2 miles) to a
crossroads. Turn right for a short distance as the route
rounds the hillside and descends very steeply into
Countersett. Another opportunity for a rest and to cool
down can be taken by Semer Water.

From Semer Water the route climbs along a narrow
lane for 2¹/₂km (¹/₂ mile) to Stalling Bush. Veer left here
to follow the hillside round and climb once again to

Kidstones Fell at 558m (1,830ft). It is worth spending some time here to enjoy the wonderful sight of Wharfedale, the limestone escarpments and the surrounding dales.

Continue downhill for the remainder of this route to join the B6160. Turn right here and follow the road back to Kettlewell. From Kettlewell you can cycle back to Conistone along the narrow lane known as the Dales Way, alongside the river.

Swaledale and Wensleydale Ride

54km (34 miles)
Landranger Map 1:50,000 Sheet 98
Starting Point: Hawes Map Ref 875 898

Brief Description

A medium difficult ride incorporating some very steep hills, mostly along narrow country lanes.

The Route

From the small town of Hawes follow the sign for Muker on the left. Pass the camp site at Brown Moor over the River Ure. Go left and immediately right. Veer left again and climb up a very steep and exhausting narrow lane for 6km ($3^3/_4$ miles) to Buttertubs. You will most likely be in need of a rest at this point but the stunning view across Wensleydale will make all the effort well worthwhile.

The lane then descends quite steeply into the village of Thwaite. Turn right and head for Muker where the River Swale runs parallel with the road. Continue along this very quiet road, passing through the Dales village of Gunnerside, and in 3km (2 miles) a narrow lane heads right over the River Swale. Follow this and turn immediately left along the south side of the Swale into Grinton.

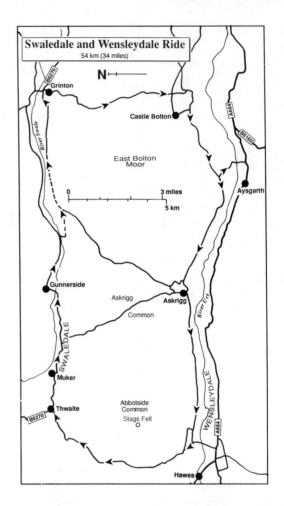

Swaledale and Wensleydale Ride
54 km (34 miles)

N

0   3 miles

5 km

Grinton
Castle Bolton
East Bolton Moor
Aysgarth
Gunnerside
Askrigg
Askrigg Common
SWALEDALE
Muker
Thwaite
Abbotside Common
Stags Fell
WENSLEYDALE
Hawes
River Swale
River Ure
B6270
A684
B6160
B6270
A684

From Grinton the route goes right at the Bridge Hotel
along a lane signposted to Redmire. You will need your
low gears now — the Yorkshire Dales are very beautiful
but as you have chosen to view them on mountain bikes
then you are going to realise this the hard way. However,
your legs will probably stand the pace much better than
the mechanics of a car.

A typical view of Swaledale from a quiet country lane

An unrelenting climb to Redmire Moor is quickly followed by a descent into Redmire via Castle Bolton and a welcome respite. From Redmire turn right along the narrow road to Carperby. At the end of the village take the road on the left for a short deviation to Aysgarth Falls. A small fee is payabl, but the falls are worth a visit.

Back on the lane to Carperby take the left turn into Wensleydale along the lane that runs just above the River Ure. After 6km (3$^3/_4$ miles) the lane bears left descending fairly steeply into the hillside village of Askrigg. Passing the church on the right continue for another 7$^1/_2$km (4$^1/_2$ miles) until a lane on the left crosses over the river returning you back to Hawes.

Malham and Halton Gill Ride

48km (30 miles)
Landranger Map 1:50,000 Sheet 98
Starting Point: Malham Map Ref 903 631

Brief Description *This ride begins with a very steep, although relatively short climb out of Malham heading for the nature trail that runs alongside the north side of Malham Tarn. This is very much an up and down route, the hills at times are almost excruciatingly difficult.*

The Route From the stony track which forms the nature trail, cycle to a junction and turn right up a narrow winding lane

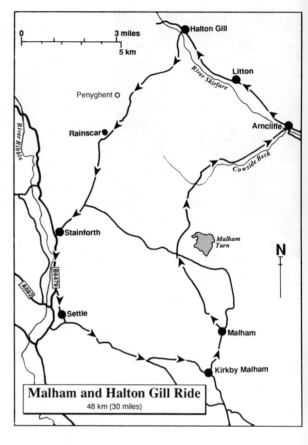

Malham and Halton Gill Ride
48 km (30 miles)

climbing gradually for 4km (2¹/₂ miles). A short distance past the turning point for Darnbrook House the lane heads very steeply downhill. Before you begin your descent into Arncliffe take time to enjoy the really spectacular views all around this part of the Yorkshire Dales.

Arncliffe is a very tiny village and on arrival there turn left at the triangle, pass a church on the right and then go left to Littondale, passing Litton Hall, to Halton Gill. This is a good place to take a break, refuel with energy bars and

The scenic beauty of Littondale

liquid in preparation for the ascent up to Penyghent House. This is a steep and uncompromising section and by the time you reach Penyghent House you will probably be in need of further refreshment.

If you can find somewhere safe to leave your bike for an hour, a walk along the Pennine Way up to Penyghent is well worth the effort.

From here the route evens out to some degree, giving fine unspoilt views again. At Rainscar a stony farm track heads right to Churn Milk Hole. Follow this, bypassing the Pennine Way, and descend very steeply into Helwith Bridge. Join the B6479 heading towards Stainforth and Settle. You can avoid going into the centre of Settle by taking a narrow lane on the left past Langcliffe. This leads to the east of Settle and you can follow this and a sign pointing to Kirkby Malham crossing High Side and Scosthrop Moor. This is another up and down section, but by this time you should be in excellent shape. Bypass Kirkby Malham church, keeping left, and return to Malham.

Chapter 6

North York Moors

Coming from the south, the best approach to the North York Moors is via the A64 from York and the A169 to Pickering or via the A170 from the west that heads across the southern section of the moors into the Vale of Pickering.

These northern moors start just inland from the resort of Scarborough and stretch westwards, dropping into the Vale of York. Extending for over 340km^2 (550sq miles) they form one of Britain's oldest national parks. This is remote, high and wild windswept moorland interspersed with picturesque market towns, small villages pertaining to the character of this part of England, as well as historic abbeys and castles.

Lying to the north-west, the Moors include the Cleveland Hills from where the River Esk runs down through a lush valley to Whitby. From the high plateau which rises to 300m (1,000ft) other streams flow south into the deep valley of the Vale of Pickering.

Helmsley and Pickering are ideal centres for the rides in this area and are also suitable locations from where to visit some of the many attractions on offer. Helmsley is a fine market town just beneath the southern rim of the moors, and its dilapidated twelfth-century castle tends to dominate the town. Rievaulx Abbey, 3km (2 miles) north-east, surrounded by wooded hills, also dates back to the twelfth century and remains one of the most magnificent monastic ruins in Britain today.

Hutton-le-Hole is one of the most attractive villages in the North York Moors. Two becks meet here beneath small bridges alongside wide greens and lanes winding past old grey cottages. The oldest building is Quaker Cottage which dates back to the seventeenth century.

The moors have been an immensely popular region with walkers over the years, the Lyke Wake Walk and the Cleveland Way are among the most walked routes in Britain. The increased popularity of off road biking means that it is now possible to experience the bracing moorland scenery from the saddles of mountain bikes along some of the bridleways and narrow lanes that cross the region.

Bike Shops

The Cycle Shop
12 Zetland Street
Northallerton
DL6 1NA
☎ 0609 77656

The Bicycle Works
144 Victoria Road
Scarborough
YO11 1LS
☎ 0723 365594

Places to Stay

Burgate House Hotel
17 Burgate
Pickering
YO18 7AU
☎ 0751 73463

'Old Manse' Guest
House
Middleton Road
Pickering
YO18 8AU
☎ 0751 76484

Vivers Mill
Guest House
Mill Lane
Pickering
YO18 8DJ

Places of Interest

North York Moors Railway
Pickering Station
North Yorkshire
YO18 7AJ
☎ 0751 72508

The North York Moors Railway is a spectacular 30km (18 mile) line which stretches between Pickering and Grosmont. It operates a steam train service offering passengers the opportunity to disembark at any of the picturesque stations along the route.
It is open daily from April to end of October with services running on regular timetables.

Nunnington Hall
Helmsley
North Yorkshire
☎ 04395 283

This is a large seventeenth-century manor house situated on the banks of the River Rye. It has been a much-loved family home since 1562 with its magnificent hall, family bedrooms, nursery and visiting maids' room. The visitor is free to wander around the hall and also to view the famous Carlisle collection of twenty-two minature rooms which is displayed in the attics at the hall. Open: April to October usually 12noon-6pm.

Ryedale Folk Museum
Hutton-le-Hole
York
YO6 6UA
☎ 07515 367

This famous open-air museum features an extensive folk park of reconstructed historical buildings, housing collections of exhibits on the life and work of ordinary people through the ages. There are twelve buildings, all with displays and regular craft demonstrations.
Open: Easter to October 10.30am-5.30pm daily.

The Ryedale Festival
Detailed festival brochures are available from:
The Festival Office
Ryedale House
Malton
North Yorkshire
YO17 0HH
☎ 0653 600666 ext 268

This is an annual event which takes place over seventeen exciting days, usually from the last week of July until the second week of August. The festival usually presents around fifty professional arts events from a variety of venues, from villages and isolated moorlands chapels to the grandeur of Castle Howard, Settrington Orangery and Nunnington Hall. Among the arts that take place are music, theatrical events, talks, readings, literary luncheons and films.

North York Moors National Park
The Old Vicarage
Bondgate
Helmsley
York
YO6 5BP
☎ 0439 70657

Perhaps one of the best places you can visit to find out about all attractions in this part of the country is the National Park Visitor Centre in Helmsley. There is information about the special nature of the countryside as well as places to view and an audio-visual presentation. Open: April to October 11am-5pm.

Ryedale and Cleveland Way Ride

52km (32 miles)
Landranger Map 1:50,000 Sheet 100
Starting Point: Helmsley Map Ref 603 837

Brief Description *The first part of the route tends to be mostly uphill but evens out around Coxwold to give a very pleasant ride through this aprt of the Yorkshire Moors.*

The Route This ride starts in Duncombe park just to the west of Helmsley. Follow the track which goes past the castle remains and leads alongside the River Rye. Between Whinny Bank Wood and Spring Bank Wood cross the bridge, continue into Hollins Wood and as the river veers off to the right join a narrow lane by Ashberry Farm and turn left passing through a narrow woodland, climbing steeply for about 6km ($3^3/_4$ miles) to join the A170 by a picnic site. Staying on the A170 climb a short distance to Sutton Bank. A stony track is then taken on the western side of the woodland, rounding the hill, the White Horse and eventually joins a narrow road to Oldstead. This first section of the ride is particularly attractive, cycling through parks, woodland and nature trails.

From Oldstead proceed to Coxwold passing Colvil Hall and Shandy Hall. After going straight over the crossroads go over the dismantled railway and after $^1/_2$km join the bridle path on the left immediately north of Newburgh Priory. Continue on this path for 4km ($2^1/_2$ miles) passing south of Fox Foot Farm and heading in the direction of Yearsley Moor to the country road just south of Thorpe Hall. Turn right and climb the steep and narrow road that leads through the western section of Yearsley Moor to Yearsley village. Turn left at the village cross-roads passing by the south side of Martins Plantation to

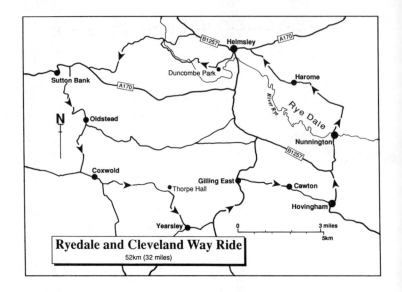

Ryedale and Cleveland Way Ride
52km (32 miles)

join the B1363. Turn left here and descend carefully for 3km into Gilling East.

On passing the church turn right and follow the sign for Cawton. This narrow country lane runs parallel with Scar Wood for almost 3km (2miles) until the lane veers sharp left. The route leaves the lane at this point to follow a well defined bridlepath known as the Ebor Way. Continue along this for another 3km (2 miles) into Hovingham.

Once in Hovingham turn left onto the B1257 and head towards Nunnington. Where the road bends to the left, take the narrow lane that cuts through Caulkleys Wood until you eventually come into the village of Nunnington. Cross the bridge over the River Rye and continue northwards for almost 2km ($1^1/_2$ miles) to the crossroads. Turn left here, riding over Riccal Moor until you arrive at the village of Harome. At the end of the village turn right by the church and then immediately left. Proceed along this lane for 3km (2 miles) until it joins the A170. Head left into Helmsley.

Cropton Forest and Spaunton Moor Ride

49km (30 miles)
Landranger Map 1:50,000 Sheet 100
Starting Point: Pickering Map Ref 798 838

Brief Description *A hilly ride on good quality moorland lanes and forest tracks.*

The Route Leave Pickering on the A170 heading west and only a few metres just outside the town turn right at a signpost marked to the Leisure Centre. You will soon leave the buildings behind as you climb gently into the country.

After about 6km ($3^3/_4$ miles) you will come to a junction where you head left towards Cropton. Take the second lane on the right and this will lead to a stony track into Cropton Forest. After cycling past Sutherland Lodges,

The ruins of Pickering Castle

follow a track going left past Spiers House and campsite. From here there is a choice of three routes, all which veer north towards Low Muffles and backtrack at different stages to Spiers Back House, leaving the forest at Hartoft

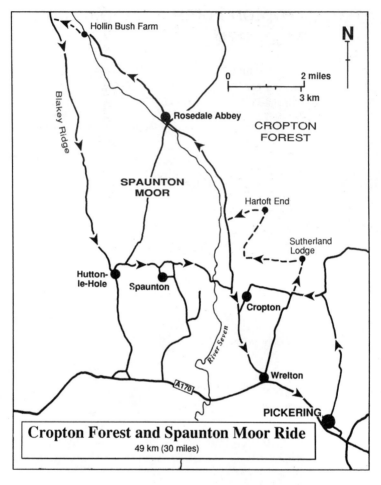

N

Hollin Bush Farm

Blakey Ridge

0   2 miles

3 km

Rosedale Abbey

CROPTON
FOREST

SPAUNTON
MOOR

Hartoft End

Sutherland
Lodge

Hutton-
le-Hole

Spaunton

River Seven

Cropton

A170

Wrelton

PICKERING

Cropton Forest and Spaunton Moor Ride
49 km (30 miles)

End. Very accurate map reading is called for in this
particular section even though the tracks are well defined.

From Hartoft End follow the road which runs just
above the River Seven to Rosedale Abbey. There is a
choice of routes from Rosedale, both along narrow lanes
which head north-west on either side of the River Seven
along Rosedale. Both eventually join farm tracks and lead

to Hollin Bush Farm. Now climb steeply from the farm to Blakey Ridge, which is a lovely place for a rest and much needed refreshments. Fine views of this part of the North York Moors can be enjoyed.

Head southwards along Blakey Ridge. The narrow road dips gradually and then quite steeply to Hutton-le-Hole. Immediately before an inn at Hutton, turn left for Lastingham and Cropton. From Cropton follow the sign back to Pickering via Wrelton.

One of the features of this ride are the very attractive limestone villages. They are ideally suited to the needs of visitors and well supplied with gift shops, cafés, pubs, various crafts and accommodation in the form of hotels, bed and breakfast and campsites.

Ryedale Ride

50km (31 miles)
Landranger Map 1:50,000 Sheet 100
Starting Point: Helmsley Map Ref 603 837

Brief
Description
The first half of the route tends to be mostly uphill but evens out around Coxwold to give a very pleasant ride through this part of the North York Moors.

The Route
This ride starts in Duncombe Park just to the west of Helmsley. Follow the track which goes past the castle ruins and leads alongside the River Rye. Between Whinny Bank Wood and Spring Bank Wood cross the bridge and continue into Hollins Wood. As the river veers off to the right, join a narrow lane by Ashberry Farm and turn left, passing through a narrow woodland and climbing steeply for about 6km ($3^3/_4$ miles) to join the A170 by a picnic site.

Staying on the A170, climb a short distance to Sutton

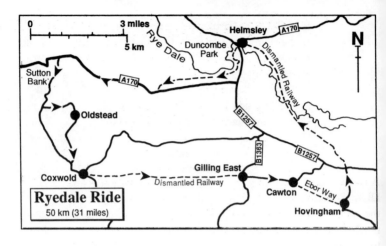

Bank. A stony track is then taken on the western side of the woodland; rounding the hill, the White Horse and eventually joining a narrow road to Oldstead.

The first section of this ride is particularly attractive, taking you through parks, woodland and nature trails.

From Oldstead proceed to Coxwold, bypassing Colvil Hall and Shandy Hall. After going straight over at the crossroads, move on to the dismantled railway for 8km (5 miles) passing Yearsley Moor on the right to Gilling East. Leave the track at Gilling, go into the village, cross the B1363 and follow the sign for Hovington. A narrow lane takes you to Cawton in the first instance and, after 3km (2 miles), leave the lane to join a stony farmers' track called 'The Ebor Way' into Hovingham village.

Once in Hovingham turn left onto the B1257. Stay on this road for about 4km (2½ miles) until you come to Scarlet Wood. Here you join the dismantled railway track once more. This crosses over the River Rye after a short distance and leads back to Helmsley.

Chapter 7

The Lake District

Although an obvious choice for some mountain bike routes, the Lake District is also one of the most sensitive of the selected regions. Due to the ever-increasing numbers of visitors to this very beautiful region of north-west England and especially the numbers of fell walkers adding to erosion problems in the mountains, the choice of routes here have been most carefully selected so as not to cause further damage to already over-populated areas. As a result, to avoid any conflict with the National Park Authorities, fell walkers and the Countryside Commission, the routes are mostly on mountain roads, passes and well defined farm and forest tracks. Even though the routes are confined mainly to these tracks, you can certainly view the Lake District and enjoy it just as much as anyone on foot.

There are no doubt several potential routes that could be devised in the region but the routes described give a fair indication of the area, providing a wide variety of scenery that is typical of the Lake District.

The region can be beautiful at any time of the year, spring and autumn being particularly good times to visit, especially if you want to avoid too many tourists. Winter can be very picturesque in the snow, but it can also be equally dreadful in damp, foggy weather.

An ideal introduction to the Lake District can be found at the National Park Centre at Brockhole which lies between Windermere and Ambleside (☎ 09662 6601). This is a special kind of information centre from where you can discover just about every aspect of the Lake District. There is also an excellent book shop, souvenir shop and café. The centre is open daily from 10am, April to early November.

Mountain Bike Shop

Lakeland Mountain Bikes
Yan Lane Ends
Elterwater
near Ambleside
LA22 9HN
☎ 05394 34464

Places to Stay

Claremount House
Compstone Road
Ambleside
LA22 9DJ
☎ 05394 33448

The Anchorage
14 Ambleside Road
Keswick
CA12 4DL
☎ 07687 72923

Fisherbeck Farmhouse
Old Lake Road
Ambleside
LA22 0DH
☎ 05394 32523

Dalkeith House
Leonards Street
Keswick
CA12 4EJ
☎ 07687 72696

Walmar Hotel
Lake Road
Ambleside
LA22 0DB
☎ 05394 32454

Hedgehog Hill
18 Blencathra Street
Keswick
CA12 4HP
☎ 07687 74386

Places of Interest

Windermere Steamboat Museum
☎ 09662 5565

Situated on the lake shore about $\frac{1}{2}$ km ($\frac{1}{4}$ mile) north of Bowness on the A592 Ambleside Road. This is a beautiful lakeside setting with a unique collection of steam, motor and sailing boats, many of them afloat and under cover. They are all in perfect working order and include one called *Dolly*; built in 1850, it is the oldest mechanically powered boat in the world. As well as a picnic area, there are also steamboat trips if the weather is suitable. There is a model boat pond, shop and refreshments.
Open: Easter to October 10am-5pm daily.

Adrian Sankey
Crystal Studio Glass
☎ Ambleside 05394
33039

Situated on Rydal Road, Ambleside, this is an open workshop with a distinctive collection of both traditional and contemporary lead crystal studio glass. Work is carried out in front of visitors with the molten glass being shaped into many diffferent forms. Among the items are delightful perfume bottles, bowls and vases, drinking vessels, period lamps and atmospheric lighting. Open: daily 9am-5.30pm.

Hayes Garden World
Ambleside
☎ 05394 33434

Located on Lake Road between Ambleside village and Waterhead, Hayes Garden World presents thousands of plants, flowers, shrubs, trees, and bushes providing a breathtaking multitude of colours throughout. There are extensive gift and garden areas, a crystal-palace plant house, coffee lounge and pine village. Open: daily except Christmas Day, Boxing Day and New Year's Day.

Lakeside and
Haverthwaite
Railway
☎ Newby Bridge
05395 31594

Based near Newby Bridge at the southern end of Lake Windermere, hard working steam locomotives haul comfortable trains from Haverthwaite Station for $5^1/_2$km ($3^1/_2$ miles) through contrasting lake and river scenery of the Leven Valley. At Lakeside connections are made with Windermere cruises for Bowness and Ambleside. Open: Easter and daily May to September. Sunday only in October.

*Lakeland Motor
Museum*
Holker Hall
Cark-in-Cartmel
☎ 05395 58509

Situated at Holker Hall, 15 minutes from Newby Bridge on the B5278 via A590, the Lakeland Motor Museum houses a fine collection of over 100 cars, motorcycles and tractors which are set against a background of numerous displays of rare and interesting automobilia. There is a discounted ticket available which includes Holker Hall, the motor museum, park, gardens and other attractions.
Open: Easter Sunday to end of October 10am-6pm. Closed Saturdays.

Rydal Mount
near Ambleside
☎ 05394 33002

Situated off the A591, 3km (2 miles) from Ambleside and 3km (2 miles) from Grasmere, this was William Wordsworth's home from 1813 until his death in 1850. There is a fine collection of family portraits, personal possessions, first editions, and 4 acres of beautiful gardens, landscaped by the poet.
Open: 9.30am-5pm daily, March to October; 10am-4pm November to February.

*Cumberland Pencil
Museum and
Exhibition Centre*
Keswick
☎ 07687 73626

Sited just west of the town centre and past the bus station, the museum traces the history of pencil making from the discovery of Borrowdale graphite in the 1500s through the early cottage industry to modern high speed production methods. Exhibits include video presentations of pencil manufacture and the use of Derwent watercolour pencils.
Open: 9.30am-4pm daily. Closed Christmas and New Year's Day.

Coniston Ride

54km (34 miles)
Landranger Maps 1:50,000. Sheets 90 and 96
Starting Point: Elterwater Map Ref 327 047

Brief Description *A moderately difficult ride through mountain passes and narrow lanes.*

The Route From the car park at Elterwater cross the bridge going over Great Langdale Beck and take the narrow lane/farmer's track that forks right, climbing through the woodland, passing Elterwater Hall, and into the hills. After $1^1/_2$ km (1 mile) turn right onto the road to the Wrynose Pass. To those unfamiliar with this pass, it is a very narrow road situated between steep sided mountains. It contains many bends and is very steep, up and down. It is certainly more suited to biking than driving.

A view from the Wrynose Pass

After 7km ($4^1/_2$ miles) you come to Cockley Beck Bridge which nestles just below Cockley Beck Fell. Go left here towards Dunnerdale and Seathwaite. This is a lovely lane which runs alongside the River Duddon, passing between Seathwaite Fells and Harter Fell. Cycle

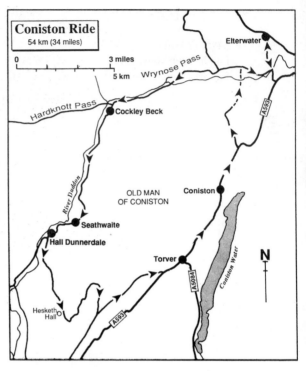

Coniston Ride

54 km (34 miles)

0 — 3 miles

5 km

Wrynose Pass

Hardknott Pass

Cockley Beck

Elterwater

A593

River Duddun

OLD MAN OF CONISTON

Coniston

Seathwaite

Hall Dunnerdale

Torver

A5084

Coniston Water

Hesketh Hall

A593

N

along this lane for 9km (5$^1/_2$ miles) to Hall Dunnerdale, keeping left at the triangle by Hall Bridge. The route then ascends very severely into the Dunnerdale Fells before descending, bypassing Scithwaite Wood, to Hesketh Hall. Cross over the River Lickle. Turning left, you climb once again up to Bracelet Moor heading for Torver.

Join the A593 passing through Torver village and on to Coniston. You can get down to Coniston at various points and will probably choose to do so anyway as the lakeside provides an idyllic place to rest and picnic.

From Coniston continue along the A593 just below Coniston Fells until you come to a right-hand bend. Take the left turn here along the narrow lane to Horse Crag and up to High Tilberthwaite. At that point a stony track leads off from the end of the road in the direction of Little Langdale Tarn. You will arrive at a climbing hut and there you turn right by a stream to a ford and footbridge. Cross the stream at this point and continue along the lane to re-join the road you took to the Wrynose Pass. Go right for a short distance, going downhill until you come to a junction, and then turn left by-passing Elterwater Lake and returning to the village.

Derwent Ride

44km (27 miles), with 14km (8³/₄ miles) extension
through Borrowdale
Landranger Map 1:50,000 Sheets 89 and 90
Starting Point: Keswick Map Ref 264 236

Brief Description
A moderately difficult ride along narrow roads and mountain passes.

The Route
From Keswick take the B5289 towards Braithwaite to join the A66. Turn left and after a short distance the route goes left by a campsite in the direction of High Lorton. This is Whinlatter Pass and it climbs steeply from Braithwaite into Thornthwaite Forest. You will come across a visitor centre about half way along this road, which also offers several forest trails/extensions.

As you come out of the forest a very narrow lane/farm track on the left just before Scaw Gill goes around the hillside to Swinside and Hopebeck to join a wider lane. Turning left here you follow the road to join the B5289 heading to Brackenthwaite, Crummock Water and Buttermere. In between the two lakes, a narrow lane on the left is taken heading towards Keswick. This proves a very stiff climb for nearly 3km (2 miles) until the lane evens out for a while before descending to a junction on the right and a tiny place called Stair. From Stair go left in the direction of Keswick again, but turn right at Swinside by the wood, keeping west of Derwent Water.

There are several places to stop for refreshments by the water on both sides. Follow the narrow lane to Grange, crossing over the River Derwent, and turn left on the B5289 back to Keswick.

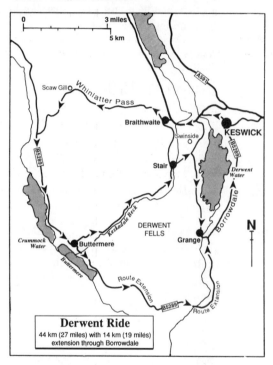

Derwent Ride
44 km (27 miles) with 14 km (19 miles)
extension through Borrowdale

The alternative road route from Buttermere continues along the B5289 and once past the lake you pass a mountain rescue post and climb quite steeply up Honister Pass for about 4km ($2^1/_2$ miles) before descending just as steeply into Borrowdale.

This is a very pretty route lined with steep-sided valleys, woodlands, crags, dales and Derwent Water itself. Stay on this road all the way back to Keswick.

Grisedale Forest and Windermere Ride

54km (34 miles)
Landranger Maps 1:50,000 Sheets 90 and 97
Starting Point: Ambleside Map Ref 367 046

Brief Description *This ride is particularly beautiful taking you through Grisedale Forest, Furness Fells and alongside two or three lakes.*

The Route Starting from Ambleside, take the A593 south-west in the direction of Coniston. Almost 2km ($1\frac{1}{4}$ miles) along the road turn left along the B5286 towards Hawkeshead. Just before Hawkeshead the road veers right, climbing through the trees on the northern edge of Grisedale Forest. After 2km ($1\frac{1}{4}$ miles) a narrow lane heads left. Follow this very beautiful ride along the eastern shores of Coniston Water for 13km (8 miles) until you come to a lane signposted Oxen Park. Go left here, climbing for a short distance into Furness Fells before descending into Oxen Park.

From there follow the sign right to Colton. At Colton take the left fork that goes around the hillside to Bouth. Turn right at Bouth to cross Rusland Pool and continue to head in the direction of the southern edge of Lake Windermere.

There are two or three roads you can use here, depending on whether you choose to make any short cuts. However, to head for Lakeside at the most south-westerly point and to follow the lane which runs parallel with the lake is arguably the most scenic route.

After about 5km (3 miles) the lane goes right at Field Head. Drop down through Bark House Wood and cycle along the shores of Windermere for a while before the lane joins the B5285. You can go right here down to the lane

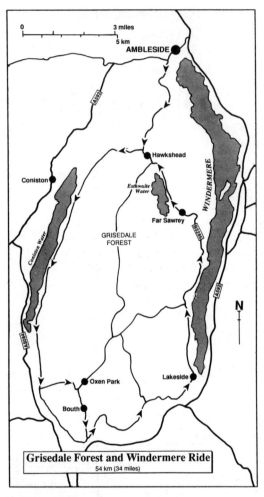

Griesdale Forest and Windermere Ride

54 km (34 miles)

and follow the track which leads from the ferry crossing point alongside the lake to High Wray; turn right onto a narrow lane which eventually joins the B5286 back to Ambleside. Alternatively, you can head left along the B5285 passing Esthwaite Water and on to Hawkeshead before rejoining the B5286 to Ambleside.

Chapter 8

The North-East

Due to the wide ranging variety of landscape in the North-East it is impossible to keep all the routes in close proximity to each other or to restrict them to one county. In order to sample this part of Britain it is necessary to spread the routes out over three counties. Durham has been chosen as perhaps the most obvious centre from where to plan the routes and to be based for the time spent in the region.

The three counties featured in this region are Tyne and Wear, Durham and Northumberland. Access to the area is by means of the A1M which runs north and south of Durham and the A69 from the west.

As a centre, Durham is one of the most visually attractive cities in Britain. Split down the centre by the River Wear which meanders down from the high Pennines, it is undoubtedly rich in both historical and architectural value. The cathedral is most impressive. Dating back to the eleventh century, it stands high over the shadows of the Wear. Durham Castle was built in 1070 and around the cathedral and the castle has grown the university which now occupies many of the buildings in the old city.

Further north from Durham the seventeenth-century Washington Old Hall, once lived in by the ancestors of George Washington, has now been tastefully renovated. A few kilometres east along the Wear a visit to the Wildfowl and Wetlands Centre is a must and as you head west along the route, Beamish Open Air Museum is located just north of Stanley.

For the other routes, you head west towards the northern fells of the Eastern Pennines. There is superb mountain biking country on the bridleways and tracks just south of the Wear Valley District through and around Hamsterley Forest. Heading north-west, there is some really beautiful moorland scenery on the route south of Hexham on the bridleways and lonely country lanes around Hexhamshire Common and the other commons.

There is certainly much to see and experience in the North-East of England. Your time spent in this area can be used to cycle on these northern fells, and to visit some of the attractions. A visit to the Northumberland Coast towards Berwick will certainly have a lasting impression upon you and it will not be long before you want to come back to this very beautiful part of England.

Bike Shop Dave Heron Cycles
6 Neville Street
Durham
☎ 091 384 0287

Places to Stay

Bridge Hotel
Croxdale
Durham City
Co. Durham
DH1 3SP
☎ 091 378 0524

Redwell Hall Farm
Edmundbyers
Shotley Bridge
Co. Durham
DH8 9TS
☎ 0270 55216

Colbrick Guest House
21 Crossgate
Durham City
Co. Durham
DH1 4PS
☎ 091 384 9585

Bankside Guest House
38 Wearside Drive
The Sands
Durham City
Co. Durham
DH1 1LE
☎ 091 384 2920

Places of Interest

The Wildfowl and Wetlands Centre
District 15
Washington
Tyne & Wear
NE38 8LE
☎ 091 4165454

The Wildfowl and Wetlands Centre is located on 100 acres of hillside not far from Sunderland. Opened 20 years ago by the late Sir Peter Scott, this is a conservation area which is home to over forty varieties of wild bird at any one time. These commonly include mallard, wigeon, pochard, tufted duck, teal, redshank, heron and lapwing. There are

ducks, geese and swans from all over the world and a special feature is the flock of Chilean flamingos. The Peter Scott Visitor Centre has picture windows looking out over a succession of ponds into the Wear Valley. The centre also contains a souvenir and coffee shop.
Open: daily 9.30am-5.30pm in summer and one hour before dusk in winter.

Beamish Open Air Museum
near Stanley
Co. Durham
DH9 0RG
☎ 0207 231811

The museum is a working example of what life in the north of England was like in the early 1900s. Visitors take a tram ride into the past to visit a turn of the century town, colliery village, working farm and railway station. Everything in the museum is authentic including the many buildings collected from all over northern England, the wallpaper in the parlour and the short-horn cattle in the fields.
Open: all year except Mondays in winter.

Finchdale Priory
Brasside
Newton Hall
DH1 5SH
☎ 091 386 3828

This is a thirteenth-century Benedictine priory situated by the River Wear. It was built around the tomb of St Godric who lived here in a hermitage until he was 105. In the fourteenth century it was used as a 'holiday home' for monks.
Open: daily from Good Friday to September 10am-6pm.

Hamsterley Forest Visitor Centre
Co. Durham
DL13 3NL
☎ 038 888312 & 646

There are exhibits in the visitor centre on forest wildlife and timber uses. Information on forest drives, walks and cycle routes is also available.
Open: all year 10am-4pm weekdays and 11am-5pm weekends.

Killhope Leadmining Centre Lanehead Upper Weardale Stanhope Co. Durham ☎ 0388 537505	Presents the most complete leadmining site in Britain. It includes a crushing mill with a 34ft diameter waterwheel, reconstructions of Victorian machinery, a railway system and miners' accommodation. Open: Easter to end of October 10.30am-5pm.
Tanfield Railway Marley Hill Gateshead NE6 5ET ☎ 0207 280643 & 091 2742002	Dating back to 1725, this is the world's oldest railway. There are passenger trains with vintage carriages, hauled by steam locomotives. Also on view is an 1854 engine shed, turntable, steam powered workshop and restoration work taking place.

Common Ride

75km (47 miles)
Landranger Map 1:50,000 Sheet 87
Starting Point: Stanhope Map Ref 991 392

Brief Description *This is quite a difficult route with steep lanes, tracks and grassy bridleways providing real mountain biking over the beautiful moors and commons around Hexham.*

The Route Leaving Stanhope on the B6278, cycle up the steep lane for 5km (3 miles) until you see a sign on the left for Blanchland. Head along this lane for 6km ($3^3/_4$ miles) going over the top of Edmundbyers Common. Drop down the hillside, cross the bridge and just after this a bridleway is signposted to your right. This is a very poorly defined track that leads across rough moorland.

Follow this trail for 7km ($4^1/_3$ miles) until you descend into Edmundbyers. Here turn left onto the B6306 from

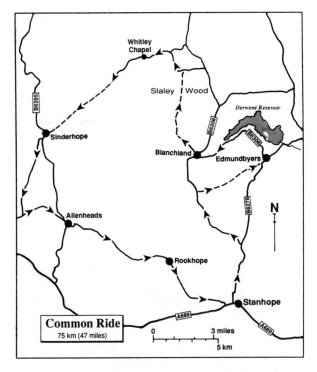

Common Ride
75 km (47 miles)

where you are rewarded with fine views of Derwent
Reservoir. Continue along the B6306 cycling close to the
south shores of the reservoir until you enter Blanchland,
aiming for the picnic parking area.

Follow the long lane up past the car park aiming for
Pennypie House. Pass through woodland and then into
moorland and, on reaching Pennypie House, bear right to
cross Blanchland Moor and go into Slaley Forest.

As soon as you enter the forest take the left track and
then go immediately right on a slightly worn bridleway.
After ¹/₂km (¹/₃ mile) of this you re-join the main forest
track which you follow in a straight line going north. The
track eventually improves and joins a lane at Holly Hill.
Turn left here and follow the lane around the edge of the

forest for a short distance, heading right past Dukesfield and then left crossing Devil's Water to Whitley Chapel.

Carry on straight over at Whitley Chapel and follow the lane to Springwell House. Three kilometres (nearly 2 miles) past Springwell House the lane ends and you then join the bridlepath that goes across Hexhamshire Common for 5km (3 miles) to Sinderhope. Ignore all tracks that join the bridleway, just carry on over the common.

At Sinderhope join the lane and bear left onto the B6295. After 2km ($1^1/_4$ miles) turn right at the signpost for Knock Shield. There is a steep drop down to cross the river and climb back up. As the road takes a sharp right turn carry on up the lane. After a short distance the lane turns into a bridleway. This is quite a difficult path to follow as you climb 200m (650ft), going in a south-westerly direc-

tion for 6km ($3^3/_4$ miles) and head left at Carshield Moor bridleway crossroads to join a lane. Turn left onto the lane and follow the sign for Allenheads.

In Allenheads follow the public parking sign and head in the direction of Rookhope, cycling on the hillside of Redburn Common and Wolfcleugh Common. Pass through Rookhope and take the left turn past the church. This will take you uphill and back into Stanhope.

An exciting track through the heather

Hamsterley Forest Ride

70km (43 miles)
Landranger Map 1:50,000 Sheet 92
Starting Point: Willington Map Ref 194 355

Brief Description   *A difficult ride on bridleways, forest tracks and moorland lanes.*

The Route   Leaving Willington on the A690 towards Crook, take the second lane on the left just past the Colliery Pub. After 2km (1¹/₄ miles) go right heading for Howden-le-Wear. Turn left onto the A689, then first right signposted Fir Tree. Pass the Australian Pub, then go first left to Witton-le-Wear.

In Witton-le-Wear go past the community centre and turn left under a bridge to the A68. Once on the A68, turn right and first left aiming towards Hamsterley. Then take the first left turn again passing Diddridge, and then turn right at the T-junction. After 2km (1¹/₄ miles) you come to another T-junction which lies opposite an unmarked bridleway. Go down the track for 50m (55yd), through the gate and following the fence. Just keep aiming for the trees in front about 2km (1¹/₄ miles) away.

At the lane turn right and the first gate on the left is a continuation of the bridleway. Keep aiming for the farm you see ahead. The bridleway brings you to North Crane Farm. Follow this track down to the lane and turn right. Cycle for 2km (1¹/₄ miles) to take the next lane on the right. You will come to some farm buildings on the left. Ignore the footpath sign and take the bridleway sign on the left. Follow this for 3km (2 miles) until you meet another lane. Here you go right, left and right again by a quarry.

Follow this narrow lane into the forest. Cross the bridge, go through a gate at the car park and climb up a narrow track to the right. This joins one of the forest trails. Follow this trail left then sharp right, crossing through the

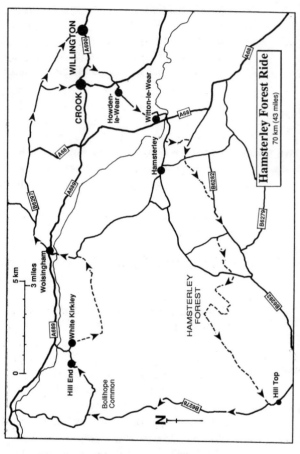

Hamsterley Forest Ride
70 km (43 miles)

open land, and head right once you have passed this section and go into the forest again. After 2km (1¼ miles) go sharp left as though you are almost coming back on yourself. Stay on this trail and it will take you straight out of the forest after about 3km (nearly 2 miles).

Cross Eggleston Common and head towards Hill Top. This is quite a difficult section to ride on, being hilly and with a poor surface. The track will take you to the B6278 and, on joining this road, go right all the way up to

Bollihope Common. After 12km (7$\frac{1}{2}$ miles) turn right at the signpost to Hill End. Cross over the river and follow the road to White Kirkley. Keep on the White Kirkley Lane as far as it goes to join the Weardale Way. Cycle along this bridleway across the fell for 2km (1$\frac{1}{4}$ miles) of rough and poorly marked track until you meet a more defined track which leads to Harthope House. Ignore the lane that takes you to the house and keep straight on following the sign for Wolsingham.

At Wolsingham you can cross the main A689 to join the B6299 and ride along that road back to Willington or you can also return to Willington by way of the A689, passing through Crook.

Railway Ride

65km (40 miles)
Landranger Map 1:50,000 Sheet 88
Starting Point: Durham Map Ref 276 426

Brief Description

This is an easy ride on specially laid tracks for cyclists close by the River Wear and River Browney.

The Route

From Durham head east on the A181, crossing over the A1M to join the B1283. At Sherburn turn left and head for West Rainton. After 4km (2$\frac{1}{2}$ miles) cross over the A690 and take the first left, dropping down into Leamside. Pass the Three Horse Shoes pub and carry straight on this road until you join the A1052. Go left and immediately right, signposted to Bournmoor. Turn right onto the A183 to Shiney Row and at Shiney Row roundabout take the road for Penshaw. Follow this road round, under the bridge and drop down at the roundabout. Turn right signposted to Fatfield, crossing over the River Wear. After the bridge turn left signposted to Washington, follow the road under

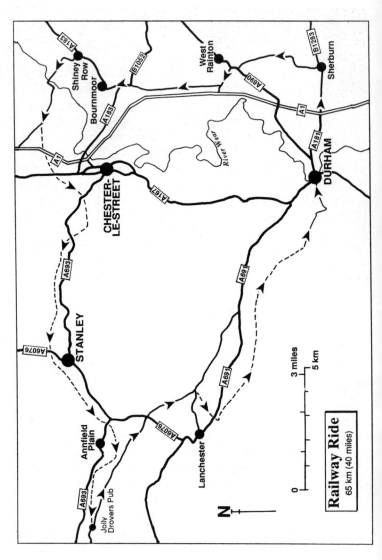

Railway Ride
65 km (40 miles)

the A182 and take the first right. Go up the hill and after 1km ($^2/_3$ mile) you will see a school on your right. Follow the road round past the school on to the bus-only link.

Durham
Castle

The entrance to the railway track is at the back of the
school yard. Go onto the rail track and turn left. This track
is well signposted and will take you all the way into
Conset. Follow it for 20km (12$^1/_2$ miles) passing Chester-
le-Street and Stanley until you come to the Jolly Drovers
pub. There take the lane signposted to Stoney Heap and
follow this straight down to the A6076. Cross over the
main road and continue along the lane heading between
Burnhope and Lanchester.

You will come to a T-junction where you go right and
immediately left on a narrow track which drops down onto
a lane, descending all the time until you come to the A691.
Go left and after a few metres go right to join the cycle
track once again. Turn left onto the track and follow this
for just over 8km (5 miles) passing Langley Park, joining
the lane which leads from Bear Park. Follow this back
towards Durham, then turn right onto the A167 and left on
the A690 to Durham centre.

Chapter 9

Kielder and the Cheviots

Sited on the edge of the Northumbria National Park and just a few miles from the Scottish border, Kielder provides a magnificent location for a choice of mountain bike rides.

Lying within the bleak rolling hills of the Northern Pennines, the region is surrounded by immense spruce forests through which several stony tracks give access for walkers, pony trekkers and, more ideally, mountain bikers.

Situated in the centre of the forest, Kielder Water is a more recent project. With a 45km (28 mile) shore line, it is the largest man-made lake and reservoir in northern Europe. It is also attracting increasing numbers of visitors who now go there to enjoy a wide range of water activities.

The rides into the forest climb at various points and, in between the many clearings marked for picnic spots, the spectacular views over the lake and towards the Cheviots are quite breathtaking.

The countryside is rich in both wildlife and historical interest. For those interested in Roman Britain there are plenty of fascinating prehistoric remains such as standing stones and Roman camps, particularly along the Roman Camp Ride, from Redesdale.

Bike Shop Robbs-Tynedale Park
      Alemouth Road
      Hexham
      Northumberland
      ☎ 0434 607788

Places	Riverdale Hall Hotel	The Cheviot
to Stay	Bellingham	Bellingham
	NE46 2JT	NE48 2AU
	☎ 0434 220254	☎ 0434 220216

Black Bull Hotel · The Pheasant Inn
Main Street · Stannersburn
Bellingham · Falstone
NE48 2JP · Kielder
☎ 0434 220226 · ☎ 0434 240382

**Places
of Interest**

*Tower Knowe Visitor
and Information
Centre*
Falstone
Hexham
☎ 0432 240398

An excellent place from where to begin your stay in Kielder, Tower Knowe provides all the information you need to know on the region. An exhibition explains all about the Kielder Water Project and how it has been developed. There is a souvenir shop, restaurant and leaflets about various activities. The Kielder Ferry leaves the jetty on regular trips around the lake, calling at a number of places on shore, usually by request.
Open: April to September 10am-6pm; October to March 10am-4pm.

*Leapish Waterside
Park*
☎ 0434 240245

About 6km ($3^3/_4$ miles) along the road from Tower Knowe, this is the main activity centre on Kielder Water. All water sports are catered for here including waterskiing, sailing, wind surfing, boating and canoeing. Craft, wet suits and life jackets can all be hired.

Kielder Castle
Visitor Centre
☎ 0434 250209

Located at the far west corner of Kielder Water in the village of Kielder, the castle was originally a hunting lodge for the Dukes of Northumberland. Kielder Castle houses a display on the history and operation of the forest and local art and craft exhibitions. Among the facilities on offer are horse-drawn wagon rides, café and picnic site.
Open: April to September daily, October, Saturday and Sunday, 10am-5pm.

Otterburn Mill
Otterburn
Northumberland
☎ 0830 20225

The Otterburn Mill has a world-wide reputation for its extensive selection of beautiful tweeds and rugs. Many interesting exhibits are on offer in the showroom including most types of tweed clothing, travel and baby rugs.
Open: Christmas to end April including Bank Holidays, 9am-5pm.

Kielder Water Ride

48km (30 miles)
Landranger Map 1:50,000 Sheet 80
Starting Point: Kielder Map Ref 626 936

Brief Description
A medium difficult ride through forest tracks.

The Route
From Kielder car park follow the road which runs along the southern shore of Bakethin Reservoir for 4km ($2^1/_2$ miles) until you come to a sign marked to Lewis Burn Picnic Site on the right. Take this stony and well defined track deep into the forest alongside Lewis Burn, crossing wooden foot bridges at the Forks and High Long House. This is quite a hilly section through a lovely part of the

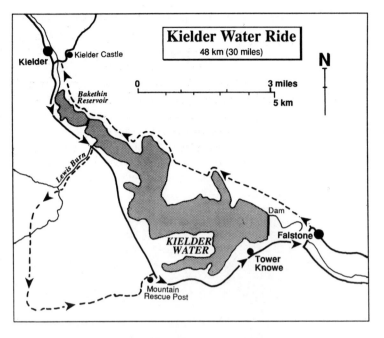

Kielder Water Ride

48 km (30 miles)

forest and, despite the number of tracks which lead to and from the main one, you cannot really go wrong.

After 14km ($8^3/_4$ miles) rejoin the road at the mountain rescue post. Turn right going past Tower Knowe Tourist Information Centre for 6km ($3^3/_4$ miles) cyling alongside Kielder Water until you come to a sign for Falstone. Go left here into the tiny village. A track just past the school heads left to Hawkehope and towards the northern side of Kielder Water.

A cycle hut just up from the car park by the dam is handily situated for any spares and from there you can either take the straight track that runs parallel with the reservoir or climb a short distance through the trees to join another stony track. Turn left here and stay on this track for about 12km ($7^1/_2$ miles) passing an old ruin at the top of an inlet from Kielder, crossing the bridge at Belling Burn,

Plashetts, Plashetts Burn and back to Kielder. Much of this section is again through forest but with fleeting glimpses of water at various forest clearings.

Throughout this ride you will notice several extensions off the main route. Because of the number of these there is no need to mention any of them in detail. However, particularly towards the latter end of the ride, if you have time and the weather conditions are in your favour then tracks which climb from Bakethin Reservoir to places like Devil's Lapful, Castle Hill, Greys Pike and the fire tower on Mount Common are well worth the extra effort.

Some climbs defeat even the fittest rider

Kielder Forest and Pennine Way Ride

53km (33 miles)
Landranger Map 1:50,000 Sheet 80
Starting Point: Kielder Map Ref 626 936

Brief Description *A classic mountain bike ride mostly on stony tracks and bridleways through Kielder Forest and the Northern Pennines. Although hilly, this is only a moderately difficult tide.*

The Route From Kielder car park follow the tarmac track past the toll point along Forest Drive. After 3½km (2 miles) the smooth tarmac changes to stony ground and is more like mountain bike terrain, at least for this region. The track is long but not too difficult, climbing for 11km (6¾ miles) through the forest alongside Ridge Burn, up to Blackhope

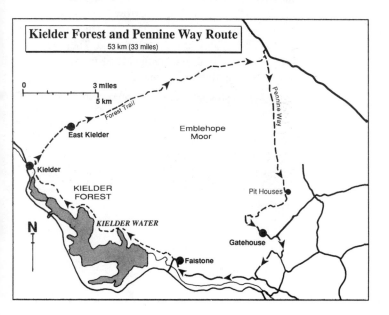

Kielder Forest and Pennine Way Route
53 km (33 miles)

0   3 miles
     5 km

Forest Trail

Pennine Way

East Kielder

Emblehope
Moor

Kielder

KIELDER
FOREST

Pit Houses

KIELDER WATER

N

Gatehouse

Faistone

Nick. There are openings in the trees and picnic spots at various points.

Once past Blackhope Nick the drive winds and descends for a further 8km (5 miles) to Blackenhopeburnhaugh. This marks the end of the forest drive. A sharp right-hand bend at the River Rede leads onto the Pennine Way. Stay on this section through the forest for 7km ($4^1/_3$ miles) until you come out onto open moorland at Gibshiel. Shortly before Gibshiel the Pennine Way itself veers left but stay on the main track continuing to Pithouses. At Pithouses the track descends right passing Highgreen Manor and as the surface improves, carry on to Gatehouse.

At this point, and depending on your fitness and state of mind, there are one or two alternatives available. You can, of course, continue on the narrow road to Redmire and follow the line of the dismantled rail track alongside the River North Tyne back to Falstone and Kielder or you can go to Burnside along a narrow lane to join a stony track into the forest. This will take you alongside Tarset Burn as far as a picnic site at Sidwood. There you head left, climbing up to the south side of the fire tower on Popes Hill and following one of the tracks to Falstone.

Alternatively, you can cross over at Gatehouse and follow the track which passes Waterhead and Highfield Burn on to Belling Burn and join the route by the north shore of Kielder Water and then head back to Kielder.

As you will notice, there are several options open here in this last section. It is hoped that this does not lead to much indecision as all of the alternatives provide attractive routes.

Roman Camp Ride

50km (31 miles)
Landranger Map 1:50,000 Sheet 80
Starting Point: Cottonshopeburntfoot Map Ref 780 016

Brief Description *A hilly and quite difficult ride on the moorland tracks of the Southern Cheviots. This ride really takes you into the midst of the Northern Pennines where, for the most part, the panoramas extend majestically for miles. Clear evidence of the Roman setttlements are seen at various points*

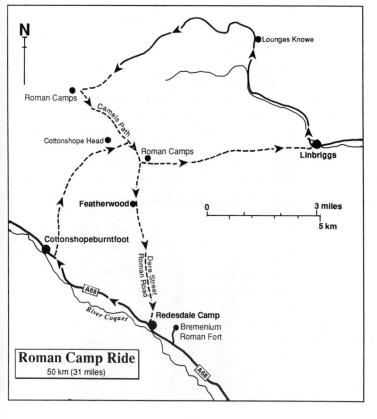

Roman Camp Ride
50 km (31 miles)

along this route. The route is hilly throughout, scenically beautiful and certainly one you will need your camera for. Major obstacles to watch out for, however, are the danger areas on the map. These areas are assigned by the Ministry of Defence as artillery ranges. The route passes carefully along part of the edge of these areas.

The Route   The first $1\frac{1}{2}$km (1 mile) of this ride climbs steadily through the forest, keeping on the left side of Cottonshope Burn. Once you are clear of the trees, it is a refreshing sight to see the fantastic views open up over the Southern Cheviot Hills.

Climbing gradually out of the forest into open moorland, pass Cottonshope Head and turn sharp right, dropping

A well equipped rider making rapid progress through the forest

down a short distance before going sharp left passing the site of a Roman camp. The route continues to drop quite steadily, passing the ruin of Ridleeshope, and eventually you will be cycling alongside Ridlees Burn to Linbriggs.

The track goes left at this point and runs parallel with the River Coquet. For the next 16km (10 miles) you will be cyling in a very steep-sided valley known as Upper Coquet Dale. It is a spectacular valley which offers fine views by the river all along this section.

Pass Bygate Hall Cottages, Barrow Burn and Carshope Plantation. The track climbs from the small forest to yet more Roman camp remains. This is a good place for a lengthy break and to regain some energy as the track now heads left to climb very steeply indeed along Camel's Path to a high point of 500m (1,650ft) from where stunning views can once again be enjoyed. There is no more climbing after this point. The track now heads down to rejoin the route cycled on earlier. Go left and immediately right, passing Roman camps again, to join another track at Featherwood. Turn right here, passing a waterfall along the Roman road known as Dere Street, and down to Redesdale camp. Turn right on the A68 back to Cottonshopeburntfoot.

Chapter 10

Brecon Beacons

The Brecon Beacons lend their name to a national park of over 800km^2 (500sq miles) taking in a trio of mountain ranges. Lying to the east are the striking green ridges of the Black Mountains, while beyond Fforest Fawr in the west you can enjoy the peace and isolation on the beautiful Black Mountain. In between the mountain ranges towns and villages nestle in the valleys with farmsteads dotting the wider landscape.

The area is easily accessible, with major road links via the M4 to London, while the A470 and the A493 head north and the M50 connects the area with the Midlands. Intercity trains to all major cities connect with local services to Abergavenny and Merthyr Tydfil.

The Brecon Beacons range is the highest in South Wales: Pen y Fan is the highest peak at 886m (2,900ft). In good weather this is a lovely mountain region to visit. In bad weather the mountains may seem forbidding but do not let this put you off. Grey, rainy and windy days are all part and parcel of the mountains.

It is suggested that you really take your time when in this region due to the sheer variety of the natural landscape you will ride through during the routes. Apart from the mountains themselves there are numerous tracks through the deep forests, fast flowing rivers, rapids, waterfalls, country parks and the spectacular illuminated Dan-yr-Ogof caves.

The principal town is Brecon. Sited on the banks of the River Usk, it lies just to the north-east of the Beacons. It is a bustling and lively place with several places of interest including the remains of a castle which is now part of the Castle of Brecon Hotel; a fine cathedral dating back to the thirteenth and fourteenth centuries; displays of country life at Brecnock Museum and an exhibition of military memorabilia at the South Wales Borders Museum.

Hay-on-Wye is a small market town. Set high above the River Wye, it nestles against the Black Mountains on the Herefordshire border. It possesses a worldwide reputation as being the town of books and stages an international festival of literature at the end of May and beginning of June. The town is full of second-hand book shops.

Mountain Bike Shop

Brook Bikes
9 Brecon Road
Abergavenny
NP7 5UH
☎ 0873 77066

Places to Stay

The Beacons Guest House
16 Bridge Street
Brecon
Powys
LD3 8AH
☎ 0874 3339

Bishops Meadow Motel
Hay Road
Brecon
Powys
LD3 9SW
☎ 0974 2051/2392

Lansdowne Hotel and
  Restaurant
39 The Watton
Brecon
Powys
LD3 7EG
☎ 0874 3321

The Old Black Lion
Lion Street
Hay-on-Wye
Powys
HR3 5AD
☎ 0497 821004

Places of Interest

Dan-yr-Ogof
Showcaves
Abercrave
Glyntawe
☎ 0639 730 284

Located midway between Brecon and Swansea, this is the largest showcave complex in western Europe. A 45-minute conducted tour of the illuminated caves allows the visitor to view the stunning limestone formations and some of the largest stalagtites and stalagmites in Britain. There is also a dinosaur park, ski slope, restaurant, museum, shop and information centre.
Open: Easter to October, daily 10am-5pm.

Henrhyd Falls

Not far from Dan-yr-Ogof Showcaves and signposted from the A4067, the waterfall here takes a 90ft unbroken plunge. There are car parking facilities and a footpath to the falls. Just a few kilometres east there are several waterfalls worth visiting on the edge of the forest just south of Ystradefellte.

The Brecon Mountain Railway Company
Pant Station
Merthyr Tydfil
Mid Glamorgan
☎ 0685 4854

About 5km (3 miles) north of Merthyr Tydfil on the A465, the Brecon Mountain Railway offers the visitor the opportunity to take a trip on one of the vintage steam locomotives through beautiful scenery into the Brecon Beacons National Park. There is a stop for a picnic or forest walk by the side of the Taff Reservoir. Also available is the chance to enter the locomotive workshop and see how old steam locomotives are repaired.

Open: most days from Easter to end of September. Phone for details.

Abergavenny Castle and District Museum
Abergavenny
Gwent
☎ 0873 4282

The castle remains date from the twelfth to the fourteenth centuries and include walls, towers and gateway. In the museum there are antiquities, rural craft tools, saddler's shop, costumes and exhibits of local history. Regular temporary exhibitions are held throughout the year.

Open: March to October, Monday to Saturday 11am-5pm, Sunday 2-5pm; November to February, Monday to Saturday 11am-4pm. Castle open daily from 8am-dusk.

Brecon Beacons Ride

53km (33 miles)
Landranger Map 1:50,000 Sheet 160
Starting Point: Brecon Map Ref 046 285

Brief Description *A truly beautiful ride with some strenuous climbs and descents on well defined bridleways, mountain and forest tracks and good quality country lanes over the Brecon Beacons.*

The Route From Brecon town centre follow the B4601 from the tourist information centre, heading left to cross the River Usk. After 1km ($^2/_3$ mile) turn left by the church and go towards the hospital by the A40. Cross over the A40 on the narrow lane that climbs quite steeply at first up the lower slopes of the Brecon Beacons.

After $3^1/_2$km (2 miles) turn right onto a well defined track that becomes a bridleway after about 2km ($1^1/_4$ miles) and climbs very sharply past Bailea onto the eastern hills of the Beacons. You cycle on the side of the steep hills passing over Craig Cwm Cynwyn. It really is spectacular biking around this region as you pass a lake to your right and drop steeply into the forest, past a picnic spot and towards Pentwyn Reservoir.

Beautiful scenery awaits the adventurous

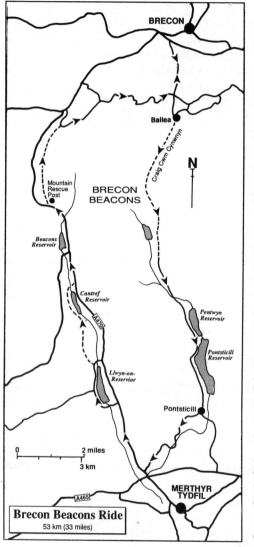

As you reach the top corner of the reservoir join the lane which leads along the west side of Pentwyn and Pontsticill Reservoirs. Follow the lane into Pontsticill and head towards the crossroads of the A470 and the A465, just outside Merthyr Tydfil. Turn right onto the A470 and ride along this road for 4km (2$^{1}/_{2}$ miles) to Llwyn-on Reservoir. Go across the dam and take the track leading up the left-hand (western) side of the reservoir. Just past the top and by the Forest Centre, follow the track which heads left and bears to the right, going through the centre of the forest to the northern end of Cantref Reservoir.

Make your way onto the A470, turning left. Pass Beacons Reservoir and continue to the Mountain Rescue Post and Storey Arms Outdoor Education Centre. A track which runs parallel with the road leads from the rescue post slanting down the hillside for 4¹/₂km (2³/₄ miles) to join a narrow lane by the River Tarrel. Turn right on the lane and follow this for 3¹/₂km (2 miles) until you come to a T-junction. Turn left there and ride downhill back to Brecon.

This is undoubtedly a ride for the accomplished mountain biker, especially on the higher parts of the Brecon Beacons. There is much variety and some fine views to be enjoyed throughout the entire route.

Fforest Fawr Ride

60km (37 miles)
Landranger Map 1:50,000 Sheet 160
Starting Point: Sennybridge Map Ref 924 288

Brief Description *This is a very difficult ride for which you will need to be in pretty good shape. The route follows well defined mountain tracks and narrow passes over what is a very beautiful and contrasting region of South Wales.*

The Route Leave Sennybridge, which is about 13km (7 miles) west of Brecon, on the A4067 to Defynnog. Just past the village of Defynnog cross over the River Senni and take the narrow track on the left for a few metres until you come to a bridleway on your right. Climb very steeply along the bridleway to the top of the hill and then descend a short distance to join a lane. Climbing once more, continue along the lane, which soon becomes a rough track again as you head towards a T-junction. Turn right onto this very narrow mountain lane for nearly 2km (1¹/₄ miles) until you come to a mountain track on the left just past the woodland.

You can also approach this track from the A4067 by following the main road from Sennybridge and turning

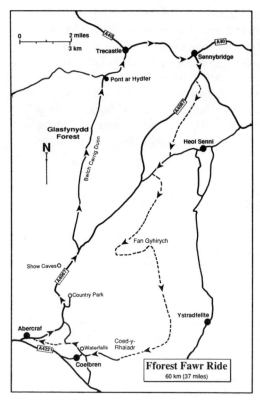

left a short distance opposite Cray Reservoir.

The track climbs very steeply up the side of the woodland and into the mountains. Heading in a southerly direction, aim towards the next plantation, the track evens out for a while before climbing very steeply again to the col of Fan Gyhirych. You then cycle very carefully downhill until you come to a junction of tracks. Turn left there and head for the woodland. Follow the track right through the trees and turn right where the track forks left out into the mountains again and descend to the edge of the next forest.

Continue on the main track (a Roman Road) along the top edge of the forest, past a fire tower to join a lane which eventually takes you into Coelbren. It should be emphasised that the route through to this point is at times very severe and great care should be taken, especially on the downhill sections.

As the lane heads left into Coelbren village, bear right past the Henrhyd Falls car park and descend along the narrow lane towards Abercraf. As you come to the A4067 turn right to follow the line of the river past Craig-y-nos

Country Park, the Dan-yr-Ogof showcaves and past Glyntawe. Cross the bridge over the River Tawe and take the next lane that comes into view on the left. Follow this mountain lane heading north towards Glasfynydd Forest. Once again, there are some extreme uphill sections on this lane. They do ease off as you go through the forest and eventually descend to Pont ar Hydfer by the River Usk.

Ignore all tracks that either join or head off the main track through the mountains and the forest. When you arrive at the junction at Pont ar Hydfer turn right to Trecastle. Once in Trecastle, go right again onto the A40 back to Sennybridge.

Black Mountains Ride

65km (40 miles)
Landranger Map 1:50,000 Sheet 161
Starting Point: Hay-on-Wye Map Ref 228 420

Brief Description *A fairly difficult ride which is very demanding at times on sections over the Black Mountains. It follows well defined bridleways and narrow mountain passes which, because of the steep slopes, need care and concentration.*

The Route Leave Hay-on-Wye on the narrow lane that heads off the B4350 just south of the junction with the B4348. You are going to need plenty of energy for this ride as the first 8km (5 miles) climb very steeply up the slopes of the Black Mountains. Follow the lane passing Tack Wood on your right to the point where the lane becomes known as the Gospel Pass.

Take some time for a well earned breather before a very long but gradual descent into the Vale of Ewyas. The mountain slopes are very steep on both sides of the pass and care is needed as you continue downhill. As you

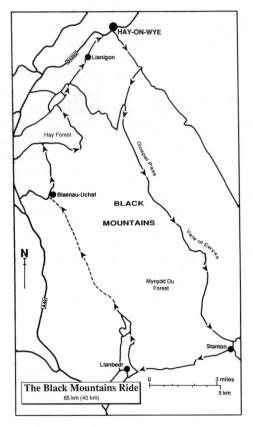

The Black Mountains Ride
65 km (40 km)

proceed along the lane, just keep following the line of the River Hondu all the way to the tiny village of Stanton.

Take the road that heads right by the telephone box in Stanton and pass through the narrow woodland. Cross over the River Fawr and turn left towards Llanbedr. You do not actually go into Llanbedr as the village is on the other side of the river. So follow the road around to the right and north back into the mountains.

6km (3³/₄ miles) from Llanbedr the lane comes to an end in a small plantation. Here you join the bridlepath that

A dusting of snow on Skirrid Fawr, Black Mountains

angles very steeply up the mountain for 4km (2¹/₂ miles) to a junction with some other tracks. Fork sharp left on the bridleway and follow the track that heads right and fork right again across the hillside and descend quite steeply towards Blaenau-Uchaf.

This is a very difficult section of the route. You are constantly surrounded by steep slopes on both sides of the track so obviously much care is needed here.

Once on the lane at Blaenau-Uchaf, turn right and follow this north for 4km (2¹/₂ miles) to a crossroads. Turn right there onto a pass which heads round the hillside towards the northern slopes of the mountains and then bears left passing Hay Forest and heading down to a T-junction. Turn right and stay on this road passing through Llanigon to join the B4350 and return to Hay-on Wye.

Chapter 11

Pembrokeshire

It is not just the mountainous regions of Britain that provide the most rugged and beautiful landscape on which to put mountain bikes to the ultimate test. There are also some spectacular rocky coastlines around Britain's shores and, together with the nearby rolling hills and quiet country lanes, one such area is North Pembrokeshire in South-West Wales.

Much of the coastal region lies within the Pembrokeshire Coast National Park and although bikes cannot be taken on the 288km (178 mile) coastal path in the Pembrokeshire district, the park does boast some of the finest clifftop scenery in Europe. There are several extensions from the routes which lead to the coast and it may even be worth your while parking your bike somewhere to walk along the clifftops to view some of the sandy coves, the forbidding cliffs, coastal flowers and a vast population of noisy sea birds.

Cardigan, Fishguard and Goodwick are the principle towns for the routes chosen in this region. Fishguard and Goodwick are in fact twin towns sited on either side of Fishguard Bay. Here is the main terminus for the South Wales railway line to London and also the ferries which provide a gateway to southern Ireland. Fishguard's Welsh name is Abergwaun, the mouth of the River Gwaun, a gentle stream that winds its way along the Gwaun Valley. Parts of the area are designated Sites of Special Interest and the valley is the haunt of the otter and raven. Fishguard itself lies on top of a steep hill, while Lower Fishguard is a picturesque port and pretty fishing harbour.

Cardigan is a market town which straddles the Teifi on an ancient, seven-arched bridge. Near the bridge are two towers and some walls, all that remains of a castle that was partly demolished in 1645.

Heading further north along the coast, you reach New Quay, which is one of the most attractive resorts on Cardigan Bay. Rising in terraces from the fine sands and a tiny harbour to a background of wooded hills, New Quay Head reaches a height of over 300ft and overlooks the harbour and superb bay.

St David's is Britain's smallest cathedral city and is named after St David, patron saint of Wales. The cathedral, set in a hollow below the town, dates back to the twelfth century. Again, as in other places around the Pembrokeshire Coast, there are several excellent bays with fine sands and clifftop scenery.

Mountain Bike Shop

Preseli Mountain Bikes
Parcynole Fach
Mathry
near Haverfordwest
Dyfed
SA62 5HN
☎ 0348 837709

This provides bike hire, guided tours, bike sales, self catering, weekend holidays and bed-and-breakfast accommodation. Spectacular sea canoeing trips are also available.

Places to Stay

Bryn Berwyn
Tresaith
Cardigan
Dyfed
SA43 2JG
☎ 0239 811126

The Old Vicarage Guest House
Molygrove
Cardigan
Dyfed
SA43 3BN
☎ 023 986231

Hotel Plas
Lower Town
Fishguard
Dyfed
SA65 9LY
☎ 0348 872296

Tregynon Country Farm Hotel
Gwaun Valley
near Fishguard
Dyfed
SA65 9TU
☎ 0239 820531

Places of Interest

Tregwynt Woollen Mill
Tregwynt
near Granston
☎ St Nicholas 03485 225

The mill is situated in a picturesque wooded valley 8km (5 miles) west of Fishguard and about $\frac{1}{2}$km ($\frac{1}{3}$ mile) from the Pembrokeshire coastline. The original buildings date back to the eighteenth century and have been in possession of the same family since 1912. The mill can be seen working from 9am to 5pm Monday to Friday. The mill shop is open every day except Sunday. Refreshments are also available. For directions just follow the Tregwynt and Abermawr signs from the A487 between Fishguard and Mathry.

Cardigan Wildlife Park
Cilgerran
Cardigan
☎ 0239 614449

Cardigan Wildlife Park is an unusual type of park and sanctuary with a diverse range of mammals, birds and plants. Other features include fishing on the River Teifi, nature walks and disused slate quarries. The ancient art of coracle fishing is also demonstrated regularly during the season.
Open: all year 10am-sunset.

Aberaeron Sea Aquarium and Animal Kingdom Centre
Located on the quay at Aberaeron
☎ 0545 570142

A few kilometres north east of New Quay, the centre consists of an information display of the marvellous marine life of West Wales, with live animals as well as models, preserved specimens, skeletons, photographs and video.
Open: end of March to October every day.

Aeron Express Aerial Ferry
Aberaeron
☎ 0545 571206

The Aeron Express is a re-creation of an unusual device first built in 1885 by Captain John Evans and which operated for 46 years. The ferry was re-opened in 1988 and is a unique experience.

Pembrokeshire Coast Ride 1

58km (36 miles), with 10km (6 miles) extensions to the coast.
Landranger Map 1:50,000 Sheet 145
Starting Point: Cardigan Map Ref 178 460

Brief Description *This is generally an easy ride on dismantled railtrack, well defined mountain paths and good quality country lanes over a very quiet region of South-West Wales.*

The Route From Cardigan take the A487 south, crossing the river, and by the wildlife park on the left join the dismantled rail track. Follow this south for 10km (6 miles) passing by the village of Cilgerran and to Boncath. A continuation of the track heads further south, bending round the hillside to Crymmych. Alternatively, if you choose not to stay on the track from Boncath you can follow the B4332 and join the A478 to Crymmych.

Go through this village on the A-road and just past the chapel and schools take the lane on the right for $1^1/_2$km (1 mile). Turn left at the T-junction join a path on the right after a very short distance. Follow this for 9km ($5^1/_2$ miles) climbing onto a ridge known as Mynydd Preseli until you come to the B4329. Cross over the road and continue along this path around and in between the two hills. Where a path forks to the left, keep right and descend to the next narrow lane. Cross over to join the path again heading down to cross the River Gwaun. Climb up from the river to join the narrow mountain lane that descends steeply to the A487 and turn right into Newport.

Immediately after Newport take the left turn onto a quiet lane that crosses the mouth of the River Nyfer and head in a northerly direction up Berry Hill towards the coast. Turn right at the T-junction and head along the hilly country lane that runs parallel with the coast to Molygrove.

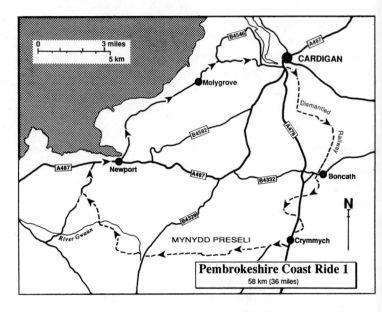

Pembrokeshire Coast Ride 1

58 km (36 miles)

From Molygrove bear left and climb the steep lane in the direction for Cardigan for 2km (1$^1/_4$ miles). Head right at the next junction, still climbing for another 1km ($^2/_3$ mile) until the lane eventually descends towards St Dogmaels, joining the B4546 and heading back to Cardigan.

Between Newport and Cardigan there are several paths and lanes which you can take to the coast. These extensions certainly provide some interesting additions to the route especially if you want to get really close to the sea. During your stay in this area it is well worth taking a look at the Pembrokeshire Coast Path. Unfortunately, you are not allowed to ride along this but the very attractive coastline offers a break from cycling and it is worth taking your camera along for a few shots.

Pembrokeshire Coast Ride 2

75km (47 miles)
Landranger Map 1:50,000 Sheet 145
Starting Point: Cardigan Map Ref 178 460

Brief
Description
This is quite a long but very easy ride along some lovely, quiet country lanes, both by the coast and over the hills inland. The hilly sections inland are not difficult, as they are mostly on good quality surfaces. Some extensions which reach the sea are optional of course and perhaps well worth the deviation for a rest.

The Route
Leave Cardigan on the B4548 heading north alongside the mouth of the River Teif to Gwbert-on-Sea. Turn right at the end of the B-road onto a narrow country lane for Verwig. Go past the two churches in Verwig and after about $1\frac{1}{2}$km (1 mile) head left in the direction of the coast. Avoiding the lane that leads off this to the coast, continue to follow the road round 2km ($1\frac{1}{4}$ miles), take the next lane on the left and descend quite sharply into Aberporth.

Joining the B4333 as you pass through Aberporth, take the first lane on the left as you ride out of the tiny resort and head for Tresaith. These are lovely, hilly country lanes to cycle on and for much of the time they give fine views over the sea. From Tresaith keep on the lanes which run parallel to the sea and head past a campsite to Penbryn. This is a very tiny place, as many of these villages are. Continue to the T-junction, turn left and after $\frac{1}{2}$km ($\frac{1}{3}$ mile) turn left again to the coastal village of Llangranog.

Leaving Llangranog on the B4321, ride for 2km ($1\frac{1}{4}$ miles), take the first country lane on the left and stay on this lane that runs by the coastline. After 4km ($2\frac{1}{2}$ miles) the lane bears right by Cwmtudu and some caves. Carry on for 2km ($1\frac{1}{4}$ miles) to a crossroads and take the lane

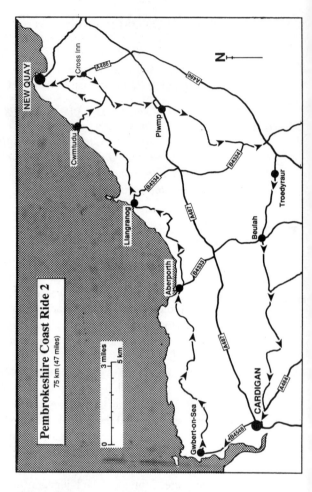

that heads left to join the A486 to New Quay.

From New Quay ride back along the A486 to Cross Inn and turn right on the narrow lane to Llwyndafydd. Just past the post office in this village turn left and head towards the A487 to Plwmp. Cross the main road and continue on the country lane for 4km (2½ miles) to a T-junction. Turn left heading towards the B4334 and join this B-road on a sharp bend after a further 2km ($1^1/_4$ miles). Keep going in a southerly direction for about 1km ($^2/_3$ mile) and take the next lane right to Troedyraur.

Turn right by the church. Cross the river and ride to Beulah. As you come to the junction of the B4333 turn right and immediately left along more hilly lanes to join the B4570. Turn right and this road will eventually take you all the way back to Cardigan.

Pembrokeshire Coast Ride 3

75km (47 miles)
Landranger Map 1:50,000 Sheet 157
Starting Point: Fishguard Map Ref 958 370

Brief Description *A fairly easy ride on good quality, quiet country lanes over the rolling hills and lovely coastal roads between Fishguard and St David's. There are some superb extensions of the route which lead to the sea, especially around St David's Head, providing some spectacular coastal scenery.*

The Route Leave Fishguard on the A40 north and head to Goodwick. Just past the junction of the A487 take the steep lane that climbs out of Goodwick onto the hillside and then take either of the two lanes that lead to Granston. From Granston continue along the hilly country lanes aiming south-west and about 3km (2 miles) after Granston follow the lane that heads right to Abercastle.

Stay on this narrow coastal lane as it weaves its way round the Pembroke hills to Trevine. After passing through the village, the lane meets the coast and continues to Llanrian. Pass through that village and ride for another 9km ($5^1/_2$ miles) to St David's. A visit to St David's Head or any other part of the coast is well worthwhile. The

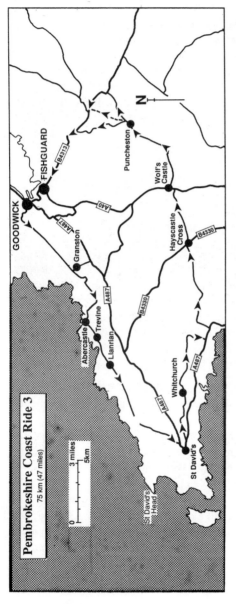

Pembrokeshire Coast Ride 3
75 km (47 miles)

scenery around this headland is stunningly beautiful.

From St David's follow the A487 south for about 1km (²/₃ mile) to join a narrow lane on the left that leads past an airfield to Whitchurch. As you go through Whitchurch take the lane that runs just north of and parallel to the A487 in the direction of a second airfield. Turn right by the edge of the airfield to join the A487. After 2km (1¹/₄ miles) take the lane that heads left on the other side of the airfield. Follow this, going over the crossroads and over the undulating hillside to Hayscastle Cross on the B4330.

Turn right and immediately left past the post office, along the lane that leads to Wolfs Castle. Turn left, then right in Wolfs Castle, over the river and climb the hill for about 3km (2 miles) to take what will be the third lane on the left to Puncheston. From Puncheston you can continue through the village and then ride between Mynydd Castlebythe and Mynydd Cilciffeth and down the slope to join the B4313. Turn left and head back to Fishguard. As you leave Puncheston on the same lane, just past the village, there are two other alternatives. One is the narrow lane which climbs steeply on your left

Pembroke-shire's rugged coastline

and heads just past the summit on the left of Mynydd Cilciffeth to join the B4313. The other route is to follow the narrow track which eventually becomes a path as it climbs and heads between Mynydd Cilciffeth and Mynydd Tre-newydd, again joining the B4313. Turn left and head back to Fishguard.

Chapter 12

Llanidloes and
The Cambrian Mountains

This area of mid Wales has been chosen because of its wild and rugged appearance. Few places in Britain can give such a sense of being deep into a mountain wilderness. With its long distances between even small towns and villages, the lonely moorland roads and bridleways separated by vast areas of rugged mountain landscape, and the dense forests, the area certainly provides a feeling of remoteness and isolation. So sparce is the population of this region that you will encounter far more sheep than people.

Hafren Forest, the beautiful Elan and Wye Valleys, the many lakes and reservoirs, the surrounding windswept moorlands and mountains combine to make this area a superb choice for the mountain rides selected.

The Cambrian Mountains are accessible from the A483 and the A470 from the north and the A470 and A44 to the south.

These mountains will never be as popular as places like Snowdonia or the Brecon Beacons, where the higher and more dramatic peaks will always attract more visitors. In the Cambrian Mountains few peaks exceed 600m (2,000ft), the highest being Plynlimon at 752m (nearly 2,500ft). This region offers a less intense, more lonely wilderness to explore and discover.

The scenery has changed considerably since the 1890s in this region. Valleys have been flooded to satisfy demands for water and the growing need for timber has resulted in areas of conifer forests on barren hills where the soil has always been too thin for cultivating purposes. So those new man-made lakes and forests have presented an extra dimension to the landscape.

Llanidloes, despite being a fairly small town, is perhaps the best centre for the rides in the region. Its close proximity to the mountains and forests has always made it a favourite centre in the past with climbers and walkers. It is within easy reach of the Plynlimon heights or the sources of the Rivers Wye and Severn.

Bike Shop
Clive Powell Mountain Bikes
The Mount
East Street
Rhayader
Powys
☎ 0597 810585

Places to Stay

Black Lion Hotel
Llangurig
Powys
SY18 6SG
☎ 0551 5223

The Old Vicarage
Llangurig
Powys
SY18 6RN
☎ 05512 280

Gorphwysfa
Westgate Street
Llanidloes
Powys
SY18 6HL
☎ 05512 3356

Severn View Guest House
China Street
Llanidloes
Powys
SY18 6AB
☎ 05512 2207

Places of Interest
Because of its remoteness and the fact that there are so few towns and villages around the Cambrian Mountains there is a lack of attractions nearby which might otherwise have been worth visiting. Having said that, this is an area where any influx of man-made tourist exhibits would not really do any justice to a very natural and unspoilt part of Britain.

The best attraction is the very wilderness that the Cambrian Mountains lend themselves to and when you are not actually cycling in the forests and across the mountains there are plenty of picnic places and other such areas either in the mountains or by the lakes and rivers.

The waterfalls by Devil's Bridge are undoubtedly among the most frequently visited attractions. The bridge, dating back to the twelfth century, is in fact the lowest of three bridges built close together over the River Mynach. This meets the River Rheidol in a series of spectacular waterfalls, the highest of which is 100m (330ft).

Rhayader is a quiet market town situated on the northern banks of the River Wye. It has become an angling, pony trekking and touring centre. It would also be ideal as a biking centre for the future. The shops offer all local products such as Welsh dressers, pottery and various other crafts.

The Elan Valley is a superb area around a chain of lakes and reservoirs and heads west from Rhayader into the surrounding mountains and moorland.

The valleys of Elan and the Wye and the source of the Severn through Hafren Forest are in themselves very beautiful places and will certainly provide you with some lasting memories once you have visited the region for a few days.

Cambrian Mountains Ride 1

60km (37 miles)
Landranger Map 1:50,000 Sheet 135
Starting Point: Devil's Bridge Map Ref 740 770

Brief Description *This is an excellent route of medium difficulty through forest tracks, mountain passes and well defined bridleways over the Cambrian Mountains and part of the Elan Valley.*

The Route Leave the waterfalls of Devil's Bridge to head south-east along the B4574 in the direction of Cwmystwyth. After 3km (nearly 2 miles) you will come to a picnic spot on the left just inside the forest. Go under the arch to join the stony track which leads north-east through the centre of the forest. You pass to the right of a fire hut and climb towards the far end of the trees. It should be noted that in

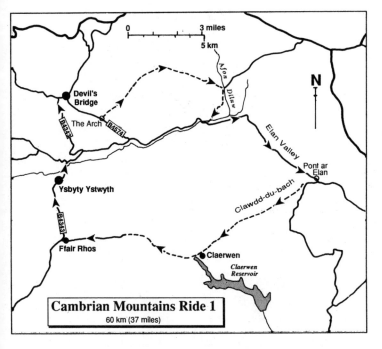

Cambrian Mountains Ride 1

60 km (37 miles)

the late autumn, around November, this forest is used by the Lombard RAC Rally.

After 4km (2¹/₂ miles) you come out into the open hillside descending along the track to a crossroads. Turn right and head for the forest on your right following the track to the far side of the trees and the Afon Diluw. Follow the track for a short distance by the side of the river until it comes out of the forest and bears right around the hill and down to the narrow mountain road.

Turn left onto the pass riding into the beautiful Elan Valley for 9km (5¹/₂ miles). About 1km (²/₃ mile) before a junction at Pont ar Elan (Map 136) a path on the right crosses the River Elan and heads in a south-west direction across the hills for 9km (5¹/₂ miles) to the corner of Claerwen Reservoir. You can follow the river down to

Claerwen or cut across to join a bridleway which eventually joins a narrow lane just north of Lyn Egnant.

This is quite a hilly and wild section of central Wales. Away from the main mountain regions you will probably have the area to yourselves whenever you decide to visit. If you try some of the routes in this region in mid-summer you will hardly meet anyone apart from a few locals.

Continue along the mountain lane for 6km ($3^3/_4$ miles) to join the B4343. Turn right to head for Ysbyty Ystwyth. Go over the River Ystwyth, through the woodland and, where the B4574 merges, bear left along the B4343 back to Devil's Bridge.

Cambrian Mountains Ride 2

45km (28 miles)
Landranger Map 1:50,000 Sheet 135
Starting Point: Ponterwyd Map Ref 748 808

Brief Description *A moderately difficult ride on the narrow mountain lanes, tracks and bridleways of the Western Cambrian Mountains. However, accurate map reading is needed once you are off the mountain lanes.*

The Route Leave Ponterwyd on the narrow mountain road that heads north and turn immediately right, crossing over the river to follow the road that runs to the right of the river and climbs gradually to the southern shores of Nant-y-moch Reservoir. The road bends to the left and crosses over the dam, following the edge of the reservoir and entering the forest.

Go through the forest as far as Llyn Nantcagl. Opposite the small lake look out for a track on the left and follow this to the end of the line of trees, moving over to the right-hand side to another track, continuing in a south-west direction as you finally come out of the trees. Fork left where the track splits in two and head for Moelglomen. Join the narrow lane which then leads to Bontgoch.

Turn left by the church and head towards the next junction. Shortly after that cross two rivers, pass a junction on the right and take the farm track which appears on the left opposite a second junction to the right. After about 1km ($^2/_3$ mile) the track deteriorates somewhat as it climbs up the hillside into the woodland and comes out by a lake.

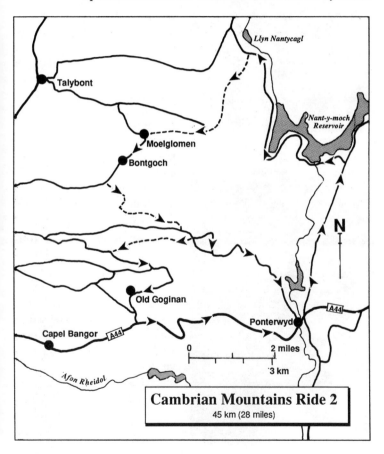

Cambrian Mountains Ride 2
45 km (28 miles)

A scenic riverside track in the Cambrian Mountains

Take the track to the right from the lake and join the very narrow lane that forks right to Lyn Pendam.

From this small lake there is a choice of routes you can follow. One is to turn left at the lake and continue to Lyn Blaennelinawr on the lane back to Ponterwyd. Alternatively, just the other side of Lyn Pendam, follow the forest track that eventually drops onto a lane and leads into Pen-bont Rhydybedddau. Take the first left there by the post office, following the lane down to the stream and the next junction. Turn left again and follow this very hilly lane round as it bends to the right to Old Goginan. Continue heading south from there to join the A44 and turn left back to Ponterwyd.

All around the area from Bontgoch, Goginan and Ponterwyd there are several extensions on bridleways and forest tracks, any one of which can be taken to enjoy the lovely mountain scenery.

'The real thing' — a genuine rough ride

Hafren Forest Ride

45km (28 miles)
Landranger Map 1:50,000 Sheet 136
Starting Point: Llanidloes Map Ref 954 845

Brief *A route of medium difficulty on narrow mountain lanes*
Description *and forest tracks that requires competent map reading*
skills.

The Route In Llanidloes take the lane that starts virtually opposite the
tourist information centre and crosses over the River
Severn. Head left on the other side of the river past the
museum. After about 1km ($^2/_3$ mile) where the lane goes
over the river, you take the right turn to head along the
north side of the Severn. Continue for 4km ($2^1/_2$ miles)
and, just before the lane crosses the river, take the right
fork which still runs along the north bank, deep into
Hafren Forest and climbing up to the picnic spot.

Very careful navigation is now required if you are to
follow this route and not get lost. You are very close to the
source of the River Severn at this point and you follow the
stony forest track that heads east from the picnic spot. It
runs just south of the water for about 3km (nearly 2 miles)
towards the edge of the forest. Just before the edge take the
track to the right. Follow this as it bends right for about
1km ($^2/_3$ mile) and take the next track which veers sharp
left. This is the outermost track in the forest. Follow this
all the way round for 9km ($5^1/_2$ miles) into the northern part
of the forest until you come out onto the narrow lane at the
north-west corner of Llyn Clywedog.

A compass may also prove useful through the forest as
there are numerous tracks that lead onto and from the main
route.

Continue heading north along the lane to join the
B4518, turning right to Staylittle. From there you can
follow the B-road south past the lake and back to

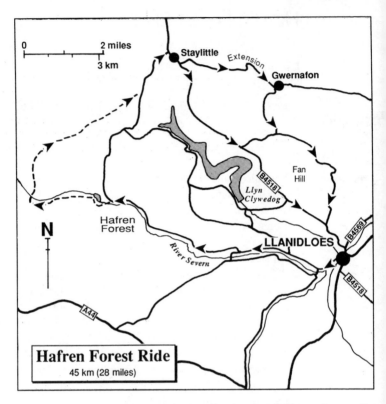

Hafren Forest Ride

Llanidloes or you can take the more hilly section on the mountain passes by taking the lane that heads east from Staylittle. It climbs steeply for $1\frac{1}{2}$km (1 mile) before providing a nice, easy descent into Gwernafon. Turn right at the junction, cycling by the stream a short distance, before turning left and immediately left again. Climb through the shallow woodland towards Fan Hill and take the next left, still climbing towards the next junction where you bare right. Stay on this lane now for the long descent back to the B4518 and into Llanidloes.

Elan and Wye Valley Ride

62km (38 miles)
Landranger Map 1:50,000 Sheet 136
Starting Point: Llanidloes Map Ref 954 845

Brief
Description
A fairly moderate route on good quality mountain passes and well defined tracks. There are some steep climbs and descents involved but these are not extreme and should not present too much difficulty.

The Route
As with the Hafren Forest ride, start by following the lane opposite the tourist information office in Llanidloes. Cross the bridge over the River Severn after 1km ($^2/_3$ mile) and continue on this lane which runs along the south bank of the river for 4km ($2^1/_2$ miles). Turn left onto the lane which heads through the woodland, past the waterfall and into the hills. Descend quite steeply to the A44 at Tyn-y-Cwm.

Turn left on to the A44 along the Wye Valley heading towards Llangurig. After $3^1/_2$km (2 miles) a narrow track on the right crosses over the Wye and heads in a south-westerly direction. After 2km ($1^1/_4$ miles) the track becomes a bridleway as it enters into the right-hand edge of the forest. Follow this track for 9km ($5^1/_2$ miles). It is a very hilly track with some steep climbs and descents as it leads into and out of the forest at various points.

Join the narrow mountain lane at Blaenycwm. Turn left and head into the beautiful Elan Valley staying on the lane for 10km (6 miles) to Pont ar Elan and the northern corner of Craig Goch Reservoir. This is a superb region and in many ways idyllic for mountain biking. From Pont ar Elan continue on the lane all the way towards Rhayader. There are a few paths and bridleways which lead off the lane and head to the reservoirs, thereby providing good places for picnics or just to relax and enjoy the peaceful surroundings.

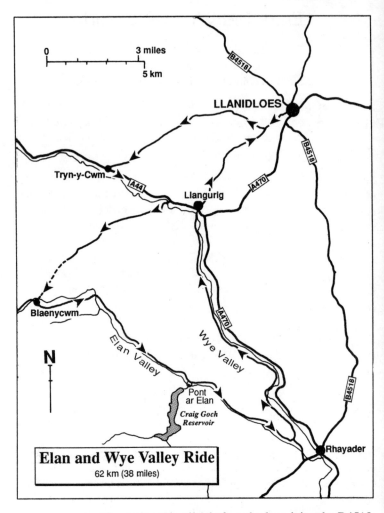

Elan and Wye Valley Ride

62 km (38 miles)

About 1km (²/₃ mile) before the lane joins the B4518 take the left turn which rounds the hillside and past the campsite to follow the line of the River Wye 15km (9 miles) north to Llangurig. As you come onto the A44 turn left and immediately right along the narrow mountain lane back to Llanidloes.

Chapter 13

Bala

Snowdonia does have some potentially interesting and very difficult mountain bike routes. However, because of its popularity with walkers and climbers, it has been decided to base these routes out of the main mountain region. Just south of Snowdonia is the very beautiful region around Lake Bala, Lake Vrynwy and the Berwyn Mountains.

Bala, a sleepy town on the north-eastern edge of Lake Bala (Llyn Tegid), is an ideal base and the three rides selected all start and finish here. Already popular as a centre for walking, it is an equally popular centre for sailing and fishing. You may well find the time to enjoy these activities during your stay.

At nearly 7km ($4^1/_3$ miles) long and $^1/_2$km ($^1/_3$ mile) wide, Lake Bala is the largest natural lake in Wales. Its cold, dark waters reach down to a depth of 46m (150ft). It is also home for the gwyniad, a white scaled salmon which lives about 25m (80ft) below the surface and is found nowhere else in Britain.

Heading south from Bala you leave civilisation behind as you make for the wilds of Penllyn Forest and across the hills to Lake Vrynwy which is surrounded by more woodland. To the east the vast extent of the Berwyn Mountains tend to dominate the horizon. These are somewhat more rounded than the jagged shaped peaks of Snowdonia and seemingly more accessible on wheels. A lovely route has been included which dissects the mountains at two points leading from and back to the River Dee.

The Berwyns are crossed again on an excellent mountain road that leads to the beautiful Tanat Valley. Despite the steep climbs and descents involved, the Berwyns are in no way as imposing as they tend to look from a distance as you first approach the region.

With the forests, lakes, mountains and river valleys, this region has a great deal to offer the mountain biker, both in terms of fine Welsh scenery and a good variety of tracks.

Bike Shop   K.K. Cycles
141 High Street
Porthmadog
☎ 0766 512310

Places to Stay   White Lion Royal Hotel
High Street
Bala
Gwynedd
LL23
☎ 0678 520314

Erw Feurig Farm
Cefnddwysarn
Bala
Gwynedd
LL23 7LL
☎ 0678 3262

Bala Lake Hotel
Bala
Gwynedd
☎ 0678 520309

Places of Interest   *Cyffdy Farm Park*
Bala
Gwynedd
☎ 0678 4271

This is the rare-breed centre of North Wales. The animals include sheep, cattle, horses, pigs, goats, rabbits, poultry, waterfowl and llama. Demonstrations of butter making and other products are given. There is a collection of old farm machinery and country bygones. Farm trail, nature trail, fishing and pony hire are all available. On occasions, you can watch sheep shearing, sheep dog handling and harp playing. You can also try your hand at donkey car rides and trailer rides.

Open: Easter to October. Winter opening by arrangement.

Bala Lake Railway
The Station
Bala
☎ 0678 4666

This narrow gauge railway runs for about 7km (4$^1/_2$ miles) from Llanuwchllyn Station, alongside Bala Lake to Bala. Three ex-Dinorwic Quarry steam engines built between 1889 and 1903 and some diesel locomotives are on view. There is also a selection of slate wagons and signals from the Lancashire and Yorkshire Railway in use. Open: late March to early October. Phone for details.

Bala Adventure and
  Watersports Centre
4 High Street
Bala
☎ 0678 521059

As a hardy bunch of reasonably fit mountain bikers, there is no reprieve from the activities offered at the Bala Adventure Watersports Centre after a day on the bikes. There are courses and activities in various outdoor sports such as rock climbing, gorge walking, windsurfing, sailing, canoeing — and mountain biking. If you like going on courses then these can be arranged for individuals and small or large groups. All activities are based in the immediate surroundings.

Berwyn, Tanat Valley and Lake Vrynwy Ride

60km (37 miles)
Landranger Map 1:50,000 Sheet 125
Starting Point: Bala Map Ref 928 362

Brief Description

An easy route, mostly on narrow mountain roads and moorland lanes. There are, of course, some hills to negotiate over the Berwyn Mountains but these are on good quality surfaces. A few forest tracks also provide some worthwhile extensions.

The Route

From Bala take the B4391 south and cross the River Dee. Head east along this quiet road, climbing into the Berwyn

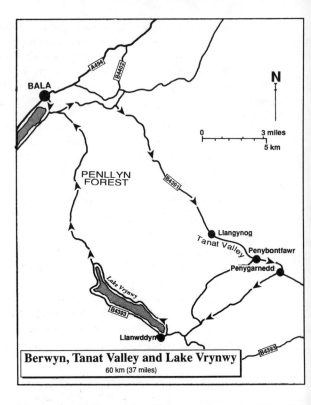

Berwyn, Tanat Valley and Lake Vrynwy
60 km (37 miles)

Mountains. You actually ride across them for 19km (12 miles), descending to the village of Llangynog. Go through the village to cross the River Tanat by a caravan site. Continue along the Tanat Valley on the B-road, passing through Penybontfawr and into Penygarnedd.

As the road bends sharply to the right take the narrow lane which heads right just before the phone box. Climb along this lane into the narrow woodland. Pass through this out into open moorland, over a cattle grid and into a larger forest to join the B4396. Turn left on the B-road and head towards Llanwddyn.

If you decide to spend some time in the forest there are several interesting extensions on good stony tracks well

140

worth taking. You can, in fact, make a detour on one or two of the forest tracks on your way to Llanwddyn.

From this village you can ride on either side of Lake Vrynwy. It is very picturesque and there are plenty of places to stop. Work your way to the top corner and take the narrow mountain pass that climbs through the woodland out into the hills. Once past the cattle grid, the pass angles down quite steeply and cuts through the middle of Penllyn Forest.

If you followed the forest track on the Penllyn Forest ride previously and you have time to spare on this route, then just to get away from the roads, try some of the other extensions that lead into the forest on both sides of the road. Some of them are circular routes and you can soon work your way back onto the road. Others lead to dead ends at the edge of the forest or join footpaths, in which case you will have to re-trace your tracks. There is much to do, however, and it is suggested that you take the time necessary to enjoy some of these extensions.

Go back on the road when you have had enough of forest tracks, then head back to your starting point in Bala.

River Dee and Berwyn Mountain Ride

70km (43 miles)
Landranger Map 1:50,000 Sheet 125
Starting Point: Bala Map Ref 928 362

Brief Description *This is a fine scenic ride which offers a variety of landscape on good mountain lanes and well defined bridleways. There are some steep climbs on the Berwyn Mountains but these should not present too much difficulty.*

The Route Leave Bala on the A494 heading east. After 2km (1$\frac{1}{4}$ miles) take the right fork along the B4401 which winds its

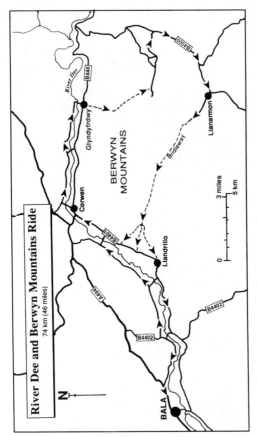

River Dee and Berwyn Mountains Ride

74 km (46 miles)

way along the north banks of the River Dee. In $4\frac{1}{2}$km (3 miles) turn left by a bridge onto the B4404. Take the first right onto a narrow lane which runs parallel with the Dee, continuing through the valley for 9km ($5\frac{1}{2}$ miles) eventually heading right to cross the river onto the B4401, joining the A5 as you ride into Corwen. Approaching the other side of Corwen turn opposite the church onto a lane which crosses over the Dee to join the B5437.

Proceed right to Carrog. Shortly after this village, where the B-road bends to the right (crossing the river) take the left turn along the narrow lane which follows the line of the river, climbing slightly up the valley before going right to cross the bridge and back onto the A5. Turn left for only a very short distance. There is a chapel on the right and at the side of this take the bridleway that climbs deep into the Berwyn Mountains. In 3km (nearly 2 miles) the track enters Ceiriog Forest. As you ride through the forest ignore other tracks that join the main route and go on to a picnic spot. When you come out of the forest continue along the narrow lane over the hills for $1\frac{1}{2}$km (1 mile) until you arrive at a T-junction. Turn left and follow this lane round the hills to join the B4500.

Head right on the B-road to Llanarmon. The B-road ends by a crossroads after crossing the River Ceiriog.

'Shall I or shan't I?'

Turn right there on a narrow lane and head north by the side of the river as far as the lane goes. It deteriorates as the river narrows and becomes a bridleway which climbs steeply into the Berwyns again. It is quite a long uphill section and shortly after passing the shooting cabin and a small plantation of trees on your right descend quite sharply towards the B4401.

Shortly after starting the descent there is a choice of two or three routes to follow. You can fork to the right and join the farm track that leads to Rhydyglafes; or bear left and as you come to a bridge over the mountain stream you can take the left fork and follow the track all the way to Llandrillo. Alternatively, follow the bridleway through woodland by the side of the stream and join a lane that brings you to the B4401 and turn left to the same village.

Head west for 6km ($3\frac{3}{4}$ miles) on the B4401 over the Dee to Llandderfel. Turn left, still along the river banks, to join the A494, turning left again and ride back into Bala.

Bala and Penllyn Forest Ride

48km (30 miles)
Landranger Map 1:50,000 Sheet 125
Starting Point: Bala Map Ref 928 362

Brief Description *Quite a difficult ride with some very steep climbs on forest tracks and narrow mountain passes. It is a superb route which includes some fine scenery over the Western Berwyn Mountains. However, accurate map skills are called for on the section through Penllyn Forest.*

The Route Leave Bala on the B4391 to cross over the River Dee, veering left round the bend and take the first narrow lane on your right that climbs steeply to Rhos-y-gwaliau. Crossing over the river just past the chapel, you join the lane that leads into Penllyn Forest. It follows the line of the river and passes a picnic spot.

You can follow this lane all the way through the forest if you choose, but a more interesting extension is taken by following the suggested route. Careful navigation is needed as there are no obvious points which can act as a guide. About 2km ($1^1/_4$ miles) after the picnic spot you cross over a river that joins the one you have been riding alongside. Shortly after that there are two tracks on your left. The first one leads to Gwern-yr-ewig, which is ignored and it is the second track you follow. It runs immediately parallel with the first track for a few metres and then heads sharp right. After going round a bend, take the next track on your right and climb along this for 4km ($2^1/_2$ miles) to the T-junction of another track. Turn left there and continue to climb out of the forest into the mountains.

As the track bears right at the high point it twists and turns its way round the hills on the edge of the forest, descending gradually and then steeply to re-join the lane. Turn left and head in the direction of Lake Vyrnwy. As

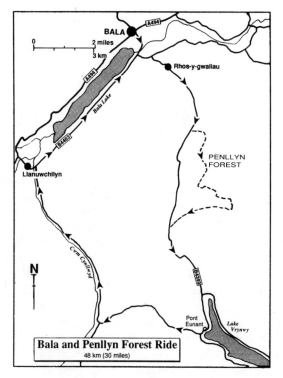

Bala and Penllyn Forest Ride
48 km (30 miles)

you reach the edge of the lake turn right onto the B4393 to
Pont Eunant. Anywhere on the banks of the lake provides
a suitable resting place and the chance for some refreshments.

Turn right over a cattle grid and climb the narrow pass
that leads through the shallow woodland and out into the
hills for 6km ($3^3/_4$ miles) to a T-junction just past another
cattle grid. Turn right and, as you begin to head north, take
time to enjoy the fine views over this very beautiful part
of the Berwyn Mountains. Continue along the narrow
road by Cwm Cynllwyd dropping gradually into
Llanuwchllyn. Turn right on the B4403, passing along the
southern shores of Lake Bala to the far corner of the lake
and follow the sign back to Bala on the B4391.

Chapter 14

New Galloway

Galloway lies in the most south-westerly region of Scotland yet, because of its situation away from the main thoroughfare, for most people it remains largely undiscovered. It stretches from the wide sands of the Solway Firth to the rocky cliffs of the Irish Sea, with barren mountains and dark forests descending to green river valleys and fertile farmland.

The area is divided by valleys, with unpolluted rivers which flow through the rich and green farmlands between the hills and the sea. It is a region of great natural beauty, fascinating attractions and extensive facilities. The variety of the south-west gives it special appeal: mountains and lochs which rival the highlands further north; rolling heathery moors, rich pastures, tumbling rivers and tranquil forests; there are also castles, towns and unspoilt eighteenth-century villages.

Many remains of ancient Neolithic and Bronze Age man lie scattered throughout the district, left by prehistoric people who chose outstanding sites for burial cairns, left strange cup-and-ring carvings on certain rocks, and were able to manipulate huge stones to make their mysterious circles.

Much of the land is occupied by the Galloway Forest Park. The routes selected in this region follow well defined tracks into the spruce forests and surrounding moorland. Such areas are Carrick Forest, The Glenkens and tracks around Lochs Clatteringshaw's, Doon and Ken.

This is a very friendly, peaceful and unhurried part of the world where people take time to help visitors. The climate here benefits from the mild influence of the Gulf Stream and in winter it is not so harsh as the more central and northern regions of Scotland.

There is plenty of interest for the naturalist in this part of Scotland. In the autumn, for instance, you can see the exciting arrival of thousands of barnacle geese at their wintering grounds by the Solway Firth, where special bird-watching tours are arranged. The huge variety of birdlife to be seen throughout the region, both coastal and inland, is a constant delight to the visitor. Also worth visiting is the Wild Goat Park and the Red Deer Range, both on the A712 west of New Galloway. As well as all this, there is Glentrool — a famous beauty spot with a winding loch, rushing waterfall and craggy, tree-lined hills.

There is no doubt that this is a superb area for mountain biking and touring. In one of the lesser known and frequented regions of Scotland there are many times when you will have the area virtually to yourself.

Bike Shop
Carrick Cycles
87 Main Street
Ayr KA8 8BU
☎ 0292 269 822

Places to Stay
Kenmure Arms Hotel
(Mr & Mrs W.J. Holberry and Mr & Mrs M.V. Swain)
New Galloway
Castle Douglas
Kirkcudbrightshire
☎ Office 06442 240. Guests 06442 360.

Leamington Hotel	The Smithy
New Galloway	Licensed Restaurant & Gift Shop
Kirkcudbrightshire	High Street
DG7 3RN	New Galloway
☎ 064 42 327	Kirkcudbrightshire
	DG7 3RN
	☎ 064 42 269

Places of Interest
Salamander Glassworks
'High Quality Handmade Glass'
Kenside Steading
St Johns Town of Dalry
Castle Douglas
Kirkcudbrightshire
DG7 3SP
☎ 06443 522

Situated just north of St Johns Town of Dalry on the A713 Ayr road, the workshop is run by Fiona and Campbell Gordon who both qualified from Scotland's only hot glass course at Edinburgh College of Art.

They produce a range of high quality, hand-made gifts and tableware with the option of a personalising engraving service. The work produced at Salamander incorporates the brilliance of lead crystal with a vast range of vibrant and exciting colours.

Open: Saturday, Sunday, Monday and Tuesday for blowing, 10am-5pm (phone for other times).

Galloway Sailing Centre
Shirmers Bridge
Loch Ken
Castle Douglas
DG7 3NQ
☎ 06442 626

Situated among the rolling hills of Galloway, the sailing centre is located 16km (10 miles) north of Castle Douglas on the A713 Ayr road. Run by Roddy and Jill Hermon, the centre runs courses to suit all ages from 8 to 80 in a variety of sailing craft. There is also a large selection of windsurfers and canoes where tuition is given if requested. Wet suits or waterproofs are available for hire. A large club room is served by a kitchen providing snacks and hot lunches. The emphasis at GSC is on everyone having fun on the water in safety.

Blowplain Open Farm
Balmaclellan
Castle Douglas
Kirkcudbrightshire
DG7 3PY
☎ 06442 206

Run by Bill and Mary Blyth Blowplain, this was awarded the best Scottish open farm in 1987. On view are various breeds of cattle, sheep, peacocks, and poultry. Conducted tours lasting about 2 hours show day to day life on a small farm, with different types of animals and their uses.

Open: daily except Saturday till end of October, tour of farm at 2pm.

Anne Hughes Pottery
Auchreoch
Balmaclellan
Kirkcudbrightshire
☎ 06442 205

Consists of a large variety of colourful hand-thrown domestic ware, individual pierced plates and bowls, as well as lustered porcelain. Visitors are welcome from May to September, 10am-6pm daily.

Southern Upland Way Ride

55km (34 miles)
Landranger Map 1:50,000 Sheet 77
Starting Point: New Galloway Map Ref 634 778

Brief
escription

A hilly route that uses lonely lanes and moorland tracks.
This is a route of medium difficulty, especially if using the
Southern Upland Way.

'he Route

Leave New Galloway on the A712 towards Dumfries.
Cross the Water of Ken and take the left turn on the A769
and left again on the A702 into St Johns Town of Dalry.
Turn right onto the B7000 and follow this road for 8km (5
miles). Once you have crossed the bridge, follow the track
which goes right, marked Southern Upland Way alongside Black Water.

he Raiders'
Road Ride
takes you
round
Clattering-
naw's Loch

After 3km (nearly 2 miles) you come to a T-junction.
Turn left there onto a lane and after 1km ($\frac{1}{2}$ mile) take the
left track up and over Culmark Hill. Continue along this
track for 4km ($2\frac{1}{2}$ miles) to join the B729. Turn right and
cycle for 6km ($3\frac{3}{4}$ miles) and as you enter the wooded area
take the first track to the right. This tends to head in a

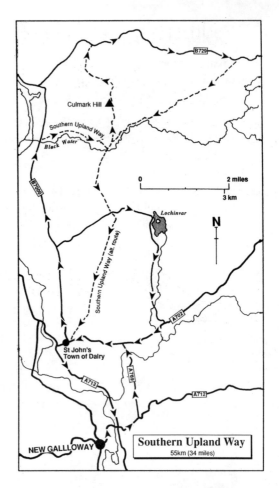

south-westerly direction and you can follow this for about 15km (9¼ miles) to re-join the A702. Alternatively, about half way down the track you can pick the Southern Upland Way route again and follow the way across the moors towards St Johns Town of Dalry.

Once on the A702, from whichever route you decide to take, head back along the A713 to New Galloway.

The Raiders' Road Ride

50km (31 miles) with variable extensions
Landranger Map 1:50,000 Sheet 77
Starting Point: New Galloway Map Ref 634 778

Brief Description *This is a route of medium difficulty with good quality lanes and tracks. There are a few climbs and descents which require some care.*

The Route Leaving New Galloway, cycle north on the A762 for 4km (2½ miles) until you come to a left turning near Glenlee Power Station. Follow this quiet lane for a short distance

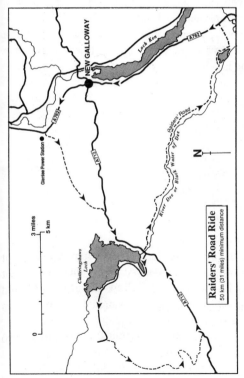

before you go left again. Cycle between Glenlee Hill and Maggot Hill into the woodland to join the A712 after 6km (3¾ miles).

Turn right and pass the Deer Museum. At the southernmost point of Clatteringshaw's Loch, turn right onto the lane which proceeds alongside the western edge of the loch. Excellent views across the loch can be enjoyed throughout this section. Towards the north-west corner of the loch the route veers left heading deep into the forest; cross under a power line and then cycle close by it for about $1\frac{1}{2}$km (1 mile) until you come to a T-junction. Turn left here and continue for a further 8km (5 miles) passing through slightly less densely populated woodland until you come once again to the A712.

Cycle east along the main road for 5km (3 miles) until you are almost opposite the entrance where you turned off for the loch. On the right-hand side of the road a track known as the Raiders' Road is taken through thick pine forest. Follow this quite hilly section for 15km (9 miles). The River Dee or Black Water runs almost parallel with the track which ends just past Stroan Loch and comes out on the A762.

You can cycle back along the A762 to New Galloway. Alternatively there are a few tracks which tend to leave Stroan Loch area and head northwards back to the starting point. It really depends on whether or not you are in a desperate hurry to leave the forest. However, accurate navigation is called for if you choose the latter option.

Carrick Forest Ride

48km (30 miles)
Landranger Map 1:50,000 Sheet 77
Starting Point: Map Ref 480 049

Brief Description *A circular route with quiet lanes and forest tracks.*

The Route Leave Dalmellington on the B741 and climb up and over to Straiton on this quiet road. At the T-junction turn left signposted Newton Stewart. Follow this hilly lane which runs alongside the Water of Girvan and after 6km ($3\frac{3}{4}$ miles) the route goes into Carrick Forest. Continue along the road for a further 6km ($3\frac{3}{4}$ miles) to Stinchar picnic site.

Turn left at Stinchar bridge and continue to follow the

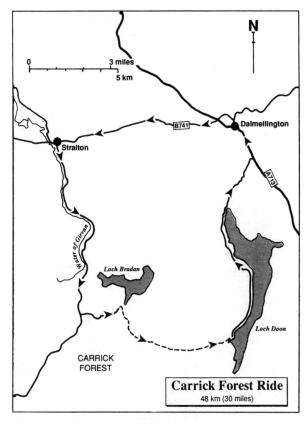

Carrick Forest Ride
48 km (30 miles)

road through the forest. After 2km (1¼ miles) a track on the left leads to Loch Bradan. You can take this track if you fancy spending some time by the loch or continue along the track on the right. As you proceed, the route always take the left forks where other tracks appear to join or venture off the main track.

Passing Loch Riecawr, keep cycling and heading for the south-west corner of Loch Doon. Staying on the western shore of the loch, bypass Loch Doon Castle and cycle for another 12km (7¾ miles) to join the A713. Turn left there and head back into Dalmellington.

Chapter 15

Peebles and Innerleithen

Peebles and Innerleithen lie very close to each other, about 40km (25 miles) south of Edinburgh and about 20km (12 miles) west of Galashiels in the Borders country.

Both towns are set in green, rolling hillside on the banks of the River Tweed. They provide ideal places for touring, walking and excellent mountain bike potential in the immediate country and moorlands.

Peebles is a quiet country town manufacturing tweeds and knitwear, and a popular place for salmon fishing along the River Tweed. It is a very historic town; the bridge, for instance, dates back to the fifteenth century. Niedpath Castle, also built in the fifteenth century, is located on a hill overlooking the Tweed. It was held by the Earl of Tweedale for Charles I in the Civil War until Cromwell's artillery battered its 11ft thick walls and forced its defenders into submission. It was later restored and sold to the Queensberry family.

Innerleithen is a village where Leithen Water meets the River Tweed and is situated on the northern edge of Elibank and Traquair Forest. It is famous for its tweed and the first tweed mill was built in 1790.

The surrounding area provided much scope for selecting routes and the four rides selected in this region give a good indication and insight into these southern Scottish hills. The rides are of varying degrees of difficulty on moorland and forest tracks and lonely country lanes.

Bike Shop   George Pennel Cycles   Open: Tuesday to Saturday
                 3 High Street   10am-5.30pm, Sunday 12noon-
                 Peebles   4.30pm.
                 EH45 8AG
                 ☎ 0721 20844

Places to Stay

Kingsmuir Hotel
Springhill Road
Peebles
EH45 9EP
☎ 0721 20151

Park Hotel
Innerleithen Road
Peebles
Peeblesshire EH45 8BA
☎ 0721 20451

The Leadburn Inn
Leadburn
West Linton
Peeblesshire EH46 7BE
☎ 0968 72952

Traquair Arms Hotel
Innerleithen
Peeblesshire
EH44 6PD
☎ 0896 830229

Places of Interest

Nether Mill
Huddersfield Street
Galashiels
☎ 0896 2091

This is a cashmere and woollen mill museum, which opened in 1983 and is sited in the Peter Anderson Mill complex. The museum provides an insight into the town's past life, involvement with the woollen trade and everyday items used in days gone by.
Open: April to October, Monday-Saturday 9am-5pm. Also open June to September, 12noon-5pm.
Mill tours are also available as is the mill shop with an excellent range of tartan and tweeds, cashmere, lambswool and mohair.

Kailzie Gardens
3km (2 miles) east
of Peebles on the
B7062
☎ 0721 20007

Kailzie Gardens consist of 17 acres of gardens surrounded by beautiful hillside and mature timber, situated on a private estate on the River Tweed. The walled garden dates back to 1812 with greenhouses, laburnum ally, shrub borders and a collection of shrub roses. There are woodland and burnside walks, a collection of waterfowl, a gift shop, art gallery and licensed tea room.
Open: daily 11am-5.30pm.

The Cornice Scottish Museum of Ornamental Plasterwork
31 High Street
Peebles

The museum is a recreation of a plasterer's casting workshop around the turn of the century and illustrates the main methods of creating ornamental plasterwork used in Scotland at that time. Plastering is available to try for yourself and protective gear is provided.

Open: April to October, 10.30am-12.30pm and 2-4pm.

Traquair House
Innerleithen

This is the oldest inhabited house in Scotland, once a pleasure ground for Scottish Kings in peaceful times and later a refuge for Catholic priests in more troubled times. It is here that Alexander I signed a charter over 800 years ago. The building contains a wealth of history and the Maxwell Stuarts have opened Traquair House for visitors to relive its unique atmosphere and history. Points worth viewing are the secret stairs, spooky cellars, books, and letters. There is also an art gallery, antiques and gift shops.

Open: April, May, June, September, 1.30-5.30pm; July, August, 10.30am-5.30pm.

Peebles Ride

45km (28 miles)
Landranger Map 1:50,000 Sheet 73
Starting Point: Peebles Map Ref 250 405

Brief Description
A combination of very quiet narrow lanes and the quiet A703 leading to Gladhouse Reservoir and then very tough climbs towards Bowbeat Hill.

The Route
Leave Peebles on the A72 towards Bigger. After 5km (3 miles) of breathtaking scenery, including Niedpath Castle, turn right onto a lane signposted Eddleston. Follow this lane for 7km (4$^1/_2$ miles) stopping to read the tourist information signposts on the way for a history of the area and about the wildlife.

A family enjoy the fun

Join the A703 at Eddlestone by the Horse Shoe Inn. Turn left and after 4km (2$^1/_2$ miles) take the right turn signed Temple. Continue up this lane until you see a rough road on your right signposted Moorfoot. Pass Gladhouse

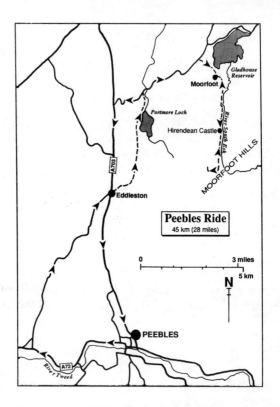

Peebles Ride
45 km (28 miles)

0   3 miles

5 km

N

Reservoir and into the Moorfoot complex. Turn right up the track just as you pass to the right of the farm buildings.

Heading south, climb up the track which comes to a dead end after 5km (3 miles) — this follows the valley of the River South Esk. Pass some remains of Hirendean Castle and return back to the reservoir. Turn back onto the lane and take the first left lane signposted to Portmore Fishery. As you come to the loch the road surface deteriorates into a stony track. Keep taking the right forks on this track. They eventually bring you back onto the A703 through a set of very impressive looking gates. Turn right on the A703 and back to Peebles.

Innerleithen
and Glenwhinnie Hill Ride

60km (37 miles), 80km (50 miles) with Glenwhinnie Hill
Landranger Map 1:50,000 Sheet 73
Starting Point: Innerleithen Map Ref 330 366

**Brief
Description**
*A gentle, longer route using mainly well surfaced, very
quiet country lanes. An option of the long, quite difficult
climb on a very rough dirt track up to Glenwhinnie Hill.*

The Route
Leave Innerleithen by the B709 south, crossing the River
Tweed, and follow the south banks of the Tweed through
Elibank and Traquair Forest until you join the A707.

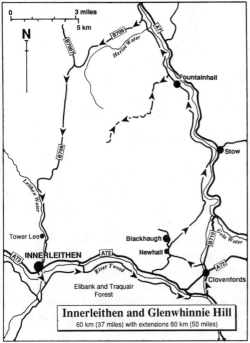

Innerleithen and Glenwhinnie Hill
60 km (37 miles) with extensions 80 km (50 miles)

Turn right on the
A707 and in a short
distance turn left onto
the B710 passing
through Cloven-
fords. Shortly after
this tiny village the
route goes left onto a
lane signposted
Newhall. Climbing
up the lane, follow it
round to the right past
Newhall and Black-
haugh towards Stow.
Follow this lane all
the way up to Foun-
tainhall keeping the
Gala Water to your
right.

If you favour the
hill climb option,
take the first road left

past Fountainhall, but there is no signpost to help you. Climb up this road and after 3km (nearly 2 miles) it changes to a track. Take the left option and go as far as you can. Then return downhill to rejoin the lane and keep on this until you turn left up the B709. Continue along this road on the north side of Heriot Water until you reach a junction. Head left near Garvald Lodge and follow the road alongside Dewar Burn, Glentress Water and Leithen Water all the way back to Innerleithen. This is a very comfortable route which most cyclists will enjoy, giving superb scenery as you cycle along the quiet lanes.

Innerleithen and Dunslair Heights Ride

38km (23 1/2 miles)
Landranger Map 1:50,000 Sheet 73
Starting Point: Innerleithen Map Ref 330 366

Brief Description *A combination of quiet roads, dirt tracks, forest paths and hill tracks. The opportunity to attempt some very difficult hill climbs in the Cardrona Forest.*

The Route Leave Innerleithen by the B709 going south past Traquair House. Turn right by a war memorial on to the B7062 signposted to Kailzie. After 3km (nearly 2 miles) a track on the left-hand side between the two cottages offers the experienced rider and map reader the chance to explore the Cardrona Forest.

Several tracks lead you back on to the B7062. These forest tracks are not really a good option for the beginner as they are not very well defined and are very steep in places. Carry on along the B7062 past Kailzie on to Peebles. Cross the River Tweed and turn right onto the

160

A72 (be careful). Follow the A72 for 3km (nearly 2 miles) and take the track to the left signposted to Glentress picnic area. Follow this stony track into the woods. At the first two forks take the left option, climbing all the time. A track joins from the left but carry straight on up. Three tracks then join from the right. Take the third one for $^1/_2$km ($^1/_3$ mile) then turn right and first left. Take the right fork after $^1/_2$km ($^1/_3$ mile) and follow this track for 3km (nearly

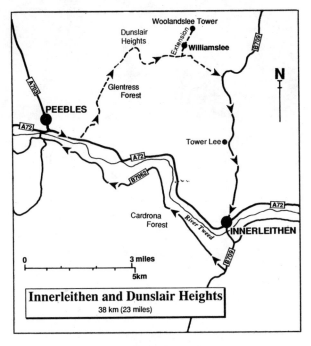

Innerleithen and Dunslair Heights
38 km (23 miles)

2 miles) to Dunslair Heights for a superb view.

You are now at the highest point of Glentress Forest. At the junction turn right and wind your way up and down until you cross the stream near Williamslee. Turn right to Leithen Lodge and go through their yards to join the B709. Turn right for Innerleithen and a well deserved downhill run into the town.

Alongside the Glentress forest

This is on the whole quite a difficult route suited mainly to the advanced rider/map reader. It is very easy to get caught up in the maze of tracks that run through Glentress Forest.

Paddock Burn Ride

Approximate distance 28km (17 miles)
Landranger Map 1:50,000 Sheet 73
Starting Point: Innerleithen Map ref 330 366

Brief Description *A very short ride on flat, quiet roads and then a short ride on rough tracks through the wooded hills.*

The Route Leave Innerleithen south on the B709. Pass Traquair House (information available) and climb gently past Newhall admiring the beautiful scenery to your right. After about 10km (6 miles) from the start follow a track to your left sign-posted to Kirkhouse South. This takes you through a gate into the forest along a stony track.

For the best views here take the left fork in the track after 3km (nearly 2 miles). This is a gentle climb and one for the beginners. An easy ride is then followed back to Innerleithen.

This is a very simple route and one you might have an hour or two for, before leaving the area.

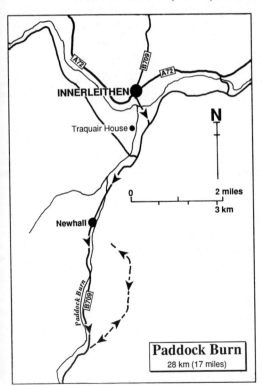

Paddock Burn
28 km (17 miles)

163

Chapter 16

Comrie and Loch Earn

Perhaps the most attractive approach to Comrie is the one from the Langside road, the B827 which leaves the Stirling to Crieff road just north of Braco and ascends the hills and winds its way through the beautiful moorland for 16km (10 miles) until it drops down into Comrie.

Comrie, taken from the Gaelic, is thought to mean 'confluence of rivers', as the Earn, Ruchill and Lednoch all converge in the village. The Dalginross Bridge, opened for traffic in 1905, replaced a temporary wooden one that was swept away in floods.

Comrie is situated on the Highland Boundary Fault, a 20,000ft deep earth fracture which divides the Lowlands and the Highlands. Movement along the fault causes occasional earth tremors in Comrie, though fortunately these are only mild ones which shake people's windows.

The towns history dates back to 3,000BC. Standing stones, stone circles, hill forts and ancient burial mounds stretching from that date to 800AD are located in the surrounding countryside.

The main thoroughfare is Drummond Street and the centre of the village faces the B827 that leads over the River Earn to Dalginross. In the centre is Melville Square and an eighteenth-century hostel named the Royal Hotel which once proved very popular with Victorian royalty and dignitaries.

The White Church is a noted landmark just across Dunira Street. Built in 1905, it is now a youth and community centre. For many years it has housed the Comrie Fortnight Exhibition. Each year, during the last week of July and the first week of August, Comrie entertains visitors and residents with a packed programme of events, shows, dances, coach tours, sports and other activities. It reaches a climax on the final

Saturday with a decorated float parade through the streets, with games and sports at Laggan Park and a carnival dance at night to round off the festivities.

One famous event in Comrie is the ancient Flambeaux procession, originally performed to drive evil spirits from the village. An annual event, the procession starts from Melville Square at midnight on New Year's Eve. Huge blazing torches are carried through the streets accompanied by a pipe band with much jollification.

Comrie and the surrounding area is without question an excellent venue for the start of mountain bike rides. The mountains, lochs and glens provide scope not just for the routes suggested in this section but for many more excursions and extensions deep into the higher mountains. The scenery is spectacular and on a sunny day, whatever time of the year, you cannot fail to enjoy the views which continually surround you.

Mountain Bike Shop

J.M. Richards
44 George Street
Perth
PH1 5JL
☎ 0738 26860

Places to Stay

Keppoch House Hotel
Perth Road
Crieff
☎ 0764 4341

Lockes Acre Hotel
Comrie Road
Crieff
☎ 0764 2526

West Lodge Holiday Homes
  and Caravan Site
Comrie
Perthshire
PH6 2LS
☎ 0764 70354

The Devil's Cauldron
  Restaurant
Dundas Street
Comrie
Perthshire
PH6 2LN
☎ 0764 70352

Places of Interest

The Glenturret Distillery
Glenturret
Crieff
Perthshire
PH7 4HA
☎ 0764 2424

Glenturret Distillery is the oldest single highland malt distillery in Scotland. It was established in 1775 but dates back to 1717. The distillery was originally in the hands of smugglers who used to smuggle the whisky to England to avoid paying taxes. The site was selected not only for its slope to the river but because there were two hills on either side which provided excellent look out points for the smugglers. The water from the River Turret is said to be as fine as any and contains all the properties needed for distilling purposes. Open: March to December, Monday to Saturday 9.30am-5.30pm. Regular guided tours are provided plus free samples of malt whiskys.

Aberfeldy Water Mill
Mill Street
Aberfeldy
PH15 2BG
☎ 0887 20803

The mill dates back to 1825. It harnesses water from the Moness Burn of the legendary Birks of Aberfeldy. The mill lade runs approximately 500yd from the Birks, underneath the town to emerge at the mill. Here the water tumbles over the powerful 15ft diameter overshot waterwheel. This powers two pairs of 54in diameter French burr stones each weighing $1^1/_2$ tons, as well as the ancillary milling equipment. Open: Easter to October Monday to Saturday 10am-6pm, Sunday 12noon-6pm.

Crieff Visitor Centre
Muthill Road
Crieff
Perthshire
☎ 0764 4014

Opened in 1985, the centre combines a glass paperweight factory and a pottery with a licensed restaurant, sales and showroom. It is possible to watch the craftsmen at work in the glass factory and pottery. Tours permit visitors to see the methods of production from start to finish. Open: 7 days a week from 9am.

Other attractions worth a visit in the region

The Weavers House and Highland Tryst Museum
Burrell Street
Crieff
PH7 4DG
☎ 0764 5202

Scottish Tartans Museum
Comrie
near Crieff
Perthshire
☎ 0764 70779

Stuart Crystal
Muthill Road
Crieff
Perthshire
☎ 0764 4004

A Ride Around Loch Earn

Basic route 40km (25 miles), with short hill climbs 48km (30 miles), or longer hill climbs 54km (34 miles)
Landranger Map 1:50,000 Sheets 51 and 52
Starting Point: Comrie Map Ref 770 220

Brief Description

A mainly easy ride on good, fast roads. However, the excursion into the mountains is extremely hard and steep as well as being on very rough tracks.

The Route

Leave Comrie on the A85 towards Lochearnhead. After 8km (5 miles) take the road left, over the bridge, signposted St Fillans Golf Club. Follow this very scenic road around the south side of the loch. Turn right into the A84 and right again at Lochearnhead onto the A85. Carry on the A85 for 8km (5 miles) until you see a caravan park and watersports centre on the right. On the left, just before

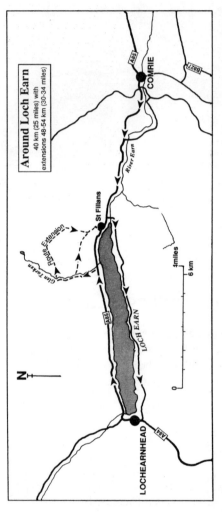

the lay-by, is a gate and sheep pen complex. Follow this track for 2km (1¼ miles), and when you have crossed the stream climb up the very difficult track that leads to the right.

After 2km (1¼ miles) this track meets another. Join this by turning right and enjoy the exhilarating ride over the top of Glen Tarken, then down into the Glen Tarken Forest. You will finally come back out onto the A85 at St Fillans. Turn left onto the A85 and head for Comrie.

For a longer extension to the mountain route, instead of taking the right turn after 2km (1¼ miles) of the track (just after the stream) carry straight on. After another 2km (1¼ miles) take the right fork and follow the track that goes along one side of the valley cut out by the stream and then loop back and follow the other side of the valley. This track (which is then joined by the track from the shorter route) leads to St Fillans. This extension is only recommended for very experienced bikers.

Loch Lednock Reservoir Ride

24km (15 miles) with 8km (5 miles) extension
Landranger Map 1:50,000 Sheet 51
Starting Point: Comrie Map Ref 770 220

**Brief
Description**

*This route is different from most of the others in this book,
as it takes you out and back on the same tracks. Do not let
this fact put you off. It is a truly beautiful area following
the valley of the River Lednock with the possibility of
several very testing rides up into the mountains. The ride
is fairly easy and on a reasonable road surface and rough
tracks.*

The Route

Leave Comrie on the road that leaves the north side of the
A85 at the sharp turn in the road in Comrie, signposted
Glen Lednock Circular Walks. There is also a telephone
box and post box at the start of the road.

Follow the main track up what is a very reasonable
standard road with passing places. Pass Lord Melville's
Monument (you can walk up the steps to see it and to enjoy
the exceptional view) and over the cattle grids. After the

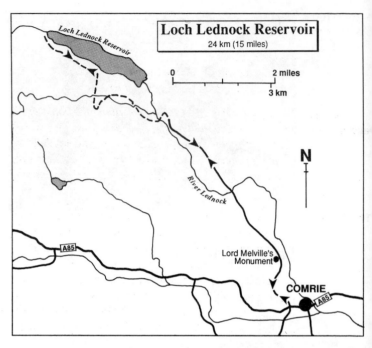

Loch Lednock Reservoir
24 km (15 miles)

fourth cattle grid take the left-hand fork down the dirt track over the wooden bridge. Follow this track for 3km (nearly 2 miles). At the junction with another track (this is not as well used) turn right and weave your way between the two hills towards the reservoir.

To extend the ride, just before you reach the banks of the loch take the track to your left that runs parallel with the water's edge. This extension is quite difficult with a couple of very steep climbs in it. After about 5km (3 miles) the track comes to a dead end and the return journey awaits you.

For a less difficult ride, instead of taking the left-hand fork over the wooden bridge, continue up the hill and straight on. After a steep descent this takes you to the loch. Unfortunately there is no track that takes you all the way round Loch Lednock Reservoir.

Glen Turret Ride

44km (27 miles)
Landranger Map 1:50,000 Sheet 52
Starting Point: Comrie Map Ref 770 220

Brief Description

A ride that starts off by taking you along the banks of the River Earn, around Crieff, a holiday town that is well worth a visit, and then up and away into the highlands of Glen Turret and a visit to Turret Reservoir. On the whole this is mostly a difficult ride; one for the experienced biker.

The Route

Leave Comrie on the B827 signposted to Braco. After 1km ($^2/_3$ mile) turn left at the T-junction down Strowan Road and follow this road along the banks of the River Earn for 10km (6 miles). Turn left onto the A822 to Crieff, then right on the A85 to Gilmerton (this avoids Crieff town centre, which can be very busy). As soon as you join the A822 take the first right, the B8062, for 3km (nearly 2 miles) and turn left on the quiet road signposted for Gilmerton.

At Gilmerton take the A822 and climb up for 3km (nearly 2 miles). On your left you will see two gates, side by side, one wooden and one metal. The wooden one has

The typical, uncompromising terrain of a Scottish glen

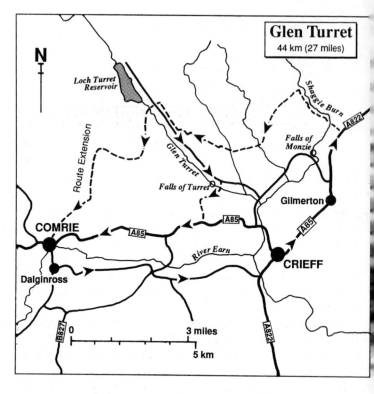

a disused cattle grid. Join the pot-holed track following the path of the Shaggie Burn. Keep your eyes open for the waterfalls and roving cattle. After 2km (1¼ miles) turn left at the T-junction and keep to this track for 7km (4½ miles) until you get to the electricity building near the head of Loch Turret.

Take the short downhill track to the left and turn left and follow this track down towards the forests for 2km (1¼ miles). At the edge of the forest take the right track over the bridge. This track weaves its way down until it joins a quiet lane after about 2km (1¼ miles). Turn right onto the lane, which takes you back onto the A85 and turn right for Comrie.

Chapter 17

Strathdon and Grantown

The area around the Grampian Mountains has been chosen as the most northerly part of Britain for these bike routes.

The Grampians form the highest mountain range in Britain, with the granite domes of the Cairngorms soaring to heights of more than 1,200m (4,000ft) above sea level. It is an immense, wild and dramatic landscape. Deep forest glens cut their way through the towering peaks above lonely lochs. The scenery which you are constantly surrounded by is unquestionably spectacular. It remains one of the most unspoilt areas of Scotland.

The best approach to the area from the south is along the A93 from Perth. This road takes you past Ballater towards Aboyne. The A939 from Ballater will lead you to Tomintoul, Grantown and in the direction of Strathdon.

The four routes are situated on the very edge of the Cairngorms massif and offer a variety of rides varying in degrees of difficulty, along river valleys, around lochs, forest tracks, leading into the hills and a distillery ride which starts at Tomintoul and takes in three whisky distilleries. This particular ride gives you the chance to visit the famous Glenlivet distilleries and to sample some of the finest malts available.

As the routes are spread out over a wide area we have included three places which are suitable centres: Aboyne, Grantown and Strathdon. Aboyne, named after the Gaelic for 'place of rippling waters' is a lovely, quiet village on the north banks of the River Dee and has always been an ideal centre and popular with outdoor sporting pursuits. Grantown lies in the woodland on the north side of the River Spey and is another popular centre particularly with skiers, walkers and anglers. Situated between the Distillery Ride and the Forest Ride, it makes for an ideal base. Strathdon is a very quiet place in the woodland which lies both sides of the River Don on the eastern slopes of the Cairngorms.

Bike Shop

B.G. Cycles
Ballater Road
Aboyne
Aberdeenshire
AB3 5HT
☎ 03398 85355/87211

A small, family-run business offering personal service and friendly atmosphere. Cycle sales and accessories.

Places to Stay

Jenny's Bothy
contact:
Michelle Scrimgeow
5 Hedge Row
Nivensknowe
Loanhead
Midlothian
EH20 9PS
☎ 09756 51446
or
Jenny Smith
Dellachuper
Corgarff
Strathdon
Aberdeenshire
AB3 8YP
☎ 09756 51449

Hazelhurst Lodge
Ballater Road
Aboyne
AB3 5HY
☎ 03398 86921

Garden Park Guest House
Garden Park
Woodside Avenue
Grantown on Spey
PH26 3JN
☎ 0479 3235

Colquhonnie Hotel
Strathdon
AB3 8UN
☎ 09756 51210

Gordon Arms Hotel
The Square
Tomintoul
Ballindalloch
Banffshire
AB3 9ET
☎ 08074 206

Places of Interest

Tomintoul Museum
The Square
Tomintoul
Ballindalloch
Banffshire
☎ 0309 73701

The museum presents a display on local history, folk life, a reconstructed farm kitchen, wildlife, climate, landscape and geology. There is also a tourist information centre.
Open: Easter to end of October, Monday to Saturday 9.30am-5.30pm, Sunday, 2-3.30pm; July and August, Monday to Saturday 9am-7pm, Sunday 11am-7pm.

Corgarff Rural Exhibition
Ordachoy
Corgarff
☎ 09756 223

Corgarff Rural Exhibition is a project set up by local people which reflects rural life and times past and present. Not only does it have memorabilia, but it is also an outlet for the sale of local crafts and produce. On display are articles such as horse-drawn sledges, original ski gear, bagpipes, farm implements and much more.
Open: June to September 6 days a week 1.30-5.30pm and on request. Opening earlier from Spring 1991.

Glenlivet Visitor Centre
Ballindalloch
Banffshire
☎ 08073 427 and 202

Guided tours are offered around the distillery in parties of no more than ten, thus ensuring that individuals are able to hear the guide and see all stages of production. Many guides speak foreign languages including French, German, Spanish and Italian. Of course, free samples of the Glenlivet 12-year-old whisky are available after the tour. An audio-visual presentation entitled 'The Ballad of Glenlivet' is also available and lasts for about 10 minutes.
Open: April to end of October, Monday to Saturday 10am-4pm.

Strathdon Herb Garden
Strathdon
Aberdeenshire
☎ 09752 343

Specialist growers and suppliers of hardy herb plants together with herb garden. Also on view are culinary and medicinal plants, seeds, books, terracotta pots and gift items. Tea room and visitor facilities are also available. Open: May to September 10am-5pm daily.

Landmark Visitor Centre
Carrbridge
10km (6 miles) north of Aviemore on the old A9
☎ Carrbridge 047 984 613

The first of its kind in Europe, the Landmark Visitor Centre presents the events of the turbulent Highland history in a three-screen audio-visual show in a dramatic permanent exhibition. Outdoor attractions include tree top trail, pine forest nature centre and trails, woodland maze, and balancing trail. The Scottish Forestry Centre tells the story of the timber industry from early times. Exhibits include steam-engine powered sawmill, 65ft viewing tower, Scottish craft and bookshop, restaurant, bar, snack bar, picnic area and plant centre.
Open: 9.30am-5.30pm in winter, and 9.30am-9.30pm in summer.

Forest Ride

43km (27 miles), with extensions 54km (33$\frac{1}{2}$ miles)
Landranger Map 1:50,000 Sheet 36
Starting Point: Nethy Bridge Map Ref 002 206

Brief Description *A fairly flat ride that covers all sorts of terrain, from a short stretch on A-roads to mud tracks in the forests around Carrbridge.*

The Route Starting from Nethy Bridge Hotel, cross the B970 and follow the lane signposted to Dulnain Bridge. After about 2km (1$\frac{1}{4}$ miles) you cross the River Spey and a dismantled railway line to join the A95. Turning left onto the main road, cycle for about 3km (nearly 2 miles) until you come to a narrow lane on the right. There is no signpost, although there is a post painted yellow at the entrance just past the cottages. The bumpy lane ends after 2km (1$\frac{1}{4}$ miles).

Heading off road into the rough

Turn left onto a better quality lane and follow the meanders of the River Dulnain. Before you get to Carrbridge turn left at Carr Cottage and follow the dirt tracks through the forest. After a few metres ignore the

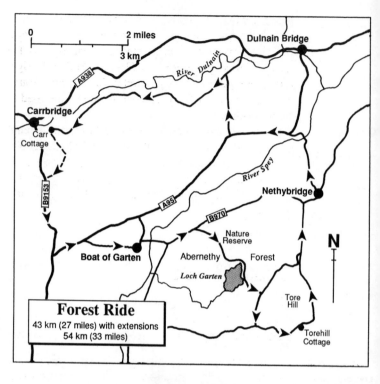

track that runs to your right. Continue until you cross the stream and leave the forest. Turn right back into the forest and after $1\frac{1}{2}$km (1 mile) you should meet the B9153.

There is another track that starts at this point leading to Docharn Farm, but it is very difficult to ride as it is steep, muddy and not well defined. This track would eventually lead you to the A95 where you could re-join the route at Boat of Garten.

Turn right at the B9153 and follow it until you reach the A95. Turn left and after $1\frac{1}{2}$km (1 mile) turn right past the school to Boat of Garten. Follow the main road going left and right through the village. Cross the river and turn left onto the B970.

After $1\frac{1}{2}$km (1 mile) enter the Abernethy Forest Nature

Reserve at the entrance signposted to Loch Garten. There are several tracks and roads around the forest. The most satisfactory is the well constructed road that goes past the loch and forks right after $3^1/_2$ km (2 miles). Follow the right fork going past Aundorach, Torehill Cottage and around the back of Tore Hill. Then continue down the road to Nethy Bridge.

If you are feeling energetic, turn off the road at Torehill Cottage and ride up the track that leads to the highest point of the hill; this is quite an exhilarating experience.

This is an easy ride with a few steep climbs; 95 per cent of the route is on good quality surfaces while 5 per cent is on mud tracks.

Distillery Ride

37km (23 miles), with extensions 54km (33 miles)
Landranger Map 1:50,000 Sheet 36
Starting Point: Tomintoul Map Ref 171 188

Brief Description   *A very scenic hilly ride using good quality, quiet roads. The paths of the River Avon and River Livet are also followed. There is the opportunity on this ride to leave the suggested route and follow one of the many trails that pass through the numerous small forests.*

The Route   Leave Tomintoul on the A939 then the B9008. Cross over the bridge, then turn sharp left. After about 1km ($^2/_3$ mile) turn left down the lane signposted to Croughly. Follow this lane that takes you through farmer's back yards for approximately 6km ($3^3/_4$ miles) and then descend until you join the B9136. There is a possible extension after 3km (nearly 2 miles). You can turn right to Glenconglass and, when you have passed the house on the left, follow the track to the left and ride up to the forest. This is well

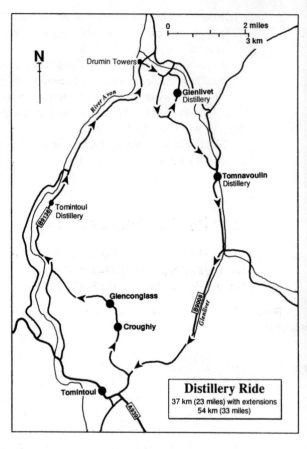

worth the ride as there are beautiful views, although unfortunately it is a dead end.

Turn right on to the B9136. Pass Tomintoul Glenlivet Distillery and follow the road for 8km (5 miles) until it bends sharp right. Drumin Towers is on your left — built in 1564, it is not open to the public. One kilometre ($^1/_2$ mile) past the tower turn right signposted Blairfindy Lodge Hotel. At the lodge you can turn left to visit the Glenlivet Distillery or carry on right down the lane to

Tomnavoulin and the Tomnavoulin Glenlivet Distillery. Turn right and follow the B9008 for 9km (5$\frac{1}{2}$ miles) to Tomintoul.

A worthwhile extension to this ride would be to turn left at Knockandhu, cycle up to Chapeltown and visit the Chapeltown Distillery. However, by this time the chances are you may well have visited enough distilleries for one day.

This is an easy ride with a few steep climbs, all on good quality surfaces.

Lochs, Forests and Castles Ride

55km (34 miles), with extensions 72km (45 miles)
Landranger Map 1:50,000 Sheet 37
Starting Point: Aboyne Map Ref 521 986

Brief Description *A very quiet but beautiful route that starts and finishes on the banks of the River Dee.*

The Route Head north on the B9094 from Aboyne. After 4km (2$\frac{1}{2}$ miles) turn right down the lane signposted Slack and turn left at the first junction. There is a church and the remains of a castle to your right. One kilometre ($\frac{2}{3}$ mile) further on, turn left again and stay on this lane until you see the sign for 'Old Town'; turn left there. This lane turns into a mud track, before joining the B9119. Turn left on the B9119 and, just before you reach Tarland, turn right down School Lane, through the estate and turn right at the bottom.

Follow this lane until you come to East Davoch. Keep on straight — onto the mud track road, through the forest and over the gate. Keeping left, go through Reinacharn Lodge. You are now back on the hard surface. Ignore the lane to your left and, to avoid the private Tillypronie, take the right fork on to the mud track until you join the A97.

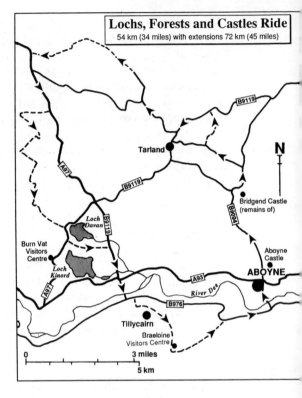

Lochs, Forests and Castles Ride
54 km (34 miles) with extensions 72 km (45 miles)

Head towards Ballater for $2\frac{1}{2}$ km ($1\frac{1}{2}$ miles) and turn right on the concrete track. Loanhead is marked on the gate. Turn left after 1km ($\frac{2}{3}$ mile) towards Kinaldie. Follow the bend past the farm and turn right down the track. At the T-junction you can turn right if you want to tackle a severe mountain track which climbs up Culbean Hill. Just follow the track straight through Bridgefoot; you can then come down into Redburn to re-join the route. This is a very difficult excursion.

To continue from the T-junction turn left on the lane; then, after 1km ($\frac{2}{3}$ mile), right to Auchnerran and left to Redburn. Turn right and after $1\frac{1}{2}$ km (1 mile) you rejoin the A97. Go right on the road and first left following the track between Loch Kinord and Loch Davan. Keep right at the junctions and leave the old Kinord House to your left. Join the B9119 and leave the Muir of Dinnet National Nature Reserve behind. Turn right and cross the A93 and the River Dee. At the T-junction turn left and then right at the signpost for Tillycairn. Carry on straight past Tillycairn. After $2^1/_2$km ($1^1/_2$ miles) turn left and drop down into Millfield. Turn right on the lane at the bottom and cross the river by the footbridge.

Follow the dirt track past the church, keep left and continue along the path by the river to the Bridge O' Ess. Turn right onto the B976 to Birsemore and then back to Aboyne. Just before the Bridge O'Ess there is a T-junction on the track. If you turn right there is a spectacular but difficult route up into the forest of Glen Tanar to Craigendinnie. These tracks will eventually lead you back onto the B976 and into Aboyne.

This is quite a hard route using narrow lanes, B-roads and mud tracks which cover about a third of the route.

River Don and Forest Ride

32km (20 miles), with extensions 41km (25 miles)
Landranger Map 1:50,000 Sheet 37
Starting Point: Strathdon Map Ref 353 132

Brief Description *Basically a simple ride that uses good quality lanes, including some valleys and steep climbs. However, the potential is there for some very serious mountain biking, taking you up dirt tracks to heights of more than 600m (2,000ft).*

The Route From Strathdon follow the road leading to Glenbuchat Lodge. This is the very narrow road which runs along the eastern side of the River Don, and on the south-western

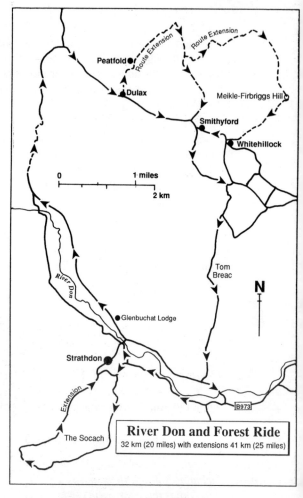

River Don and Forest Ride
32 km (20 miles) with extensions 41 km (25 miles)

side of Mid Hill. Continue along this lane for 8km (5 miles) passing Tornagawn, Torrancroy to Badenyon where the lane bends to the right, running parallel with the forest.

At a place called Dulax there is an 8km (5 mile) extension. A dirt track which heads left towards Peatfold takes you high into the mountains. Ride past Peatfold and after $2^1/_2$km ($1^1/_2$ miles) turn right, going around the back of White Hill. At the next junction turn left, going down, up and back down again. You then come to a junction and turn right this time and cycle for just over $1^1/_2$km (1 mile) taking the first right track and descending onto a small lane.

Turn right to Smithyford and then left back towards the B973, passing Belnaboth and Tom Breac. At the B973 turn left, cross the River Don, go first right and follow the banks of the Don and re-join the B973 after $5^1/_2$km ($3^1/_2$ miles). The more adventurous may like to turn left just before the B973 at the lane for Ettenbreck and cycle around the loop called Socach.

This is generally an easy route with some very steep climbs. The extensions are very difficult and you will certainly need to follow the map very carefully if you intend to stay on the suggested routes.

Where next?

Further Reading

Books (note that some of these books may not be in print)
Tim Hughes, *Cycle Tourers' Handbook*
Batsford

Rob Hunter, *Britain by Bicycle*
Weidenfeld

J. Olsen, *Mountain Biking Adventure Sport*
Salamander Hodder

Van der Plas, *The Mountain Bike Book*
Velo Press Inc, New York

Barry Ricketts, *Mountain Biking Handbook*
The Arena Press

Cyclists' Britain - (on and off highway routes)
Pan/Ordnance Survey

Crane & Gausden, *CTC Route Guide*
Penguin

Iain Lynn with others, *Off-Road Bicycle Book*
Leading Edge Press and Publishing

Richard Harries, *Cycling in the Lake District*
Moorland Publishing

Richard Harries, *Cycling in the Yorkshire Dales*
Moorland Publishing

Magazines

Mountain Biking U.K.
Bicycle Action
Bicycle
Cycle Touring & Campaigning (CTC)

Index

A Note to the Reader

We hope you have found this book informative, helpful and enjoyable. It is always our aim to make our publications as accurate and up to date as possible. With this in mind, we would appreciate any comments that you might have. If you come across any information to update this book or discover something new about the area we have covered, please let us know so that your notes may be incorporated in future editions.

As it is MPC's principal aim to keep our publications lively and responsive to change, any information that readers provide will be a valuable asset to us in maintaining the highest possible standards for our books.

Please write to:
Senior Editor
Moorland Publishing Co Ltd
Free Post
Ashbourne
Derbyshire
DE6 9BR